The Last Fidget

A desperate plea from a hidden world

Ruthie Dean

Grosvenor House
Publishing Limited

This book is published by
Grosvenor House Publishing Ltd
Link House
140 The Broadway, Tolworth, Surrey, KT6 7HT.
www.grosvenorhousepublishing.co.uk

This book is a work of fiction. Any resemblance to
people or events, past or present, is purely coincidental.

A CIP record for this book
is available from the British Library

ISBN 978-1-83975-961-1

To GRW and Teddy – the impact of their influence, they'll never know.
Special thanks to Roselyn Brooks, incredible Illustrator and friend.
And for anyone with the will – just imagine and achieve; even a pandemic can't stop creativity.

Sometimes, just sometimes, we need fantasy, not to escape but to survive in the reality.

Contents

CHAPTER ONE

The Overwhelming Trauma

All was eerily still. Curled up in a frightened ball, the strange, bony creature stirred, disoriented and confused. Thoughts raced rapidly through its bewildered mind, with immense uncertainty swirling nearby in disrupted surroundings. *What had happened?* The damp, crumbly earth felt cold beneath and with a bruised frame, an array of spindly textures unnervingly tickled at the creature's tingling skin.

With a traumatised face squashed against the uneven, bumpy ground, the creature felt engulfed in shock and pain. Dazed and feeling extremely anxious, it lay very still, occasionally breathing a slow and deliberate breath.

Tiny nostrils absorbed wafting smells from close by. Something felt familiar, though he knew not what; through the upset, utter confusion remained deep in his muddled and unsettled thoughts. *What was the recognisable smell?* With trembling anticipation, a pale, rough tongue emerged to taste the ground beneath. Weirdly, it reassured a little. Slowly, feelings of disorientation began to lift and the panicky, small creature attempted to unravel the complexities of how it got there. It listened. It listened intensely.

A cool breeze floated by and a delicate touch of light confirmed most daylight hours had gone, though the creature had no recollection of the hours before. Nearby, a faint rustling sound arose from among the tangled ground cover. Small vibrations increased in the stony ground below and all of a sudden, still dazed, he felt a sense of dread. Something was approaching, and approaching quickly. With every ounce of bravery, he opened his anxious eyes to see the cause.

With his vision gently clearing, a line of drab, brown bark bugs scurried closer and closer. Taking no interest in the weary creature, the small colony of bugs continued on their way, scavenging and scuffling through the trail of fallen leaves which lay close by. He breathed a sigh of relief as he found comfort in recalling the harmless bugs. Staying motionless, he observed them quickly pass by and head towards some bright, smelly fungi a short distance away.

With a deep breath, the timid being slowly unravelled from its bruised, coiled position. His bony fingers gradually uncurled from their tight grasp and he sat up, pausing just for a moment, before pushing himself from the ground. Large, bony feet emerged at the end of long spindly legs and sounds of breaking twigs filled the empty air around him as he stood.

Standing just a few inches in height, things began to piece together in the creature's clearing mind as his widened eyes became drawn to the upturned scene around him. Surrounded in a damp, misty atmosphere, the creature's face said it all ... complete devastation! Yesterday, everything had been so different ...

For as long as can be remembered, the Fidget family had inhabited this special and mysterious place. Now, looking at the scene, it was a world apart from the idyllic, warm and magical place the Fidgets had once enjoyed.

The diminutive being took small steps forward and surveyed the traumatised scene. As far as he could see, he was all alone. The environment seemed familiar, yet its dramatic transformation could not be explained. Typically, in the Fidget world, there would be flamboyant birds and bustling bugs filling the air with their weird and wonderful sounds, but in this one single moment, everything had gone. The hesitant Fidget searched for movement close by, grasping for any clue as to his family's whereabouts. He strained his nostrils in disbelief as the familiar smells of his numerous kinfolk wafting on the wind had gone.

Silence filled every pocket of air all around. By instinct, the Fidget feared for the rest of his family. Through nervous, narrow eyes, he forced himself to search and his vision was drawn to the central family glade.

The small, now dull glade, sat deep within Whispering Wood. All around stood huge, ancient trees. Some of the compact tree tops appeared to be tickling the grey clouds floating above as each tree swayed in its unique way. Dense shrubs and an array of unusual plant life lay subdued, all vibrancy gone, surrounding the tree bases like an irregular bumpy carpet. One could only imagine the delicate feathery ferns which previously hovered over the small pathways like silk umbrellas expecting a heavy rainstorm, as they now lay disjointed and flattened upon the scene. An irregular-shaped stream meandered across the undulating land and along its banks straggly larch trees presided over a patchwork of moss and lichen.

On this day, the constant animated sparkle from the stream had been replaced by dull, grey, semi-flowing water. Close by, small clusters of brightly coloured toadstools, in various shapes and sizes huddled together as if protecting one another in deep conversation.

The theme of a spongy, animated woodland floor flowed away from the glade itself with an undulating line leading towards dark caverns and ragged cliff faces in the distance. Beyond the caverns, at the end of another mysterious route, lined by conifers and unusual fungi stood a deep valley, with a cluster of old miner's cottages sitting side by side. In the foggy atmosphere, not far from the glade, a moss-encrusted rustic hut stood; abandoned, unloved and uninhabited. Somewhere close by, stood an old mine shaft where inhabitants of the miner's cottages would have worked, many decades ago. It had long since closed and had now been claimed by nature's continuous growth and mystical diversity.

The bewildered Fidget, known as Ash to his family, stared at the mossy rocks and pieces of flint which lay, disorganised at the muddy sides of the stream. He thought about the long grasses and pretty flowers that used to dip their thirsty roots into the glistening, flowing water.

Rubbing his weary eyes, Ash continued to stare at what was the familiar central glade. Many years before, the secretive clan chose this place as their perfect home. It seemed ideal, enriched with diversity for the little creatures to continue their life's work in relative harmony with other species.

The Fidgets always lived with a niggling thought of potential threats to their harmonious ways, from the world around them. To protect themselves, long before this shattering day, they had placed a magical charm around the glade to keep them safe. There was always a threat that perhaps another life form might disturb or even obliterate their way of life.

The complex charm had prevented harm for so long, until this day. But the fearful Fidgets always knew that a day might come when the charm would be broken. Looking at the devastation before him, Ash knew this day had arrived.

The foraging Fidgets were a very secretive species. With no real leader of the clan, they strongly believed every one of them brought something special to their meaningful existence. Being proud, they all worked extremely hard and each used their unique powers to enhance the world around them. Each Fidget would help to gather, regenerate and restore the forest's generous prizes to protect their future generations. But it was more than that. They understood the importance of nature's connections and how all species relied on others to survive and prosper. It was integral to each Fidget's core that they continued to nurture their natural habitat in the mystical realm. Future generations, of all species, depended on it. It was what drove every Fidget to work so hard.

Fragments of Ash's home were now scattered across the top of the secretive glade. An eclectic mix of mossy and dry stones, some small fungi and tufts of damp mud were strewn around. The small, neat pathway created from layered birch leaves had gone and replacing the lush, green grass mauled holes and lumps of turf with ripped up roots laid bare. At the base of the family oak tree the devastation was clear; a huge, mauled hole had been hurriedly created with dislodged roots from a frenzied attack strewn all around.

Ash tried in vain to think through the sequence of events; no matter how hard he tried, he had no recollection. *What had happened here?* He stared at the littered stones and a damp, dislodged wooden log near the disrupted stream and as he did so, a blanket of frozen panic came over him. *Where had his family gone?*

Ash walked, slowly dragging his bony feet along the dew-covered grass towards the dull stream. Trying to find the energy to place one foot in front of the other, he wondered if the magical sparkle from the stream would ever return. Close by, his saddened eyes were drawn to a flattish stone. He sat there and dipped his skinny toes into the semi-flowing water. The sun began to fade and his alert ears picked up the emerging evening birdsong from the cooling, grey sky. Even the birds seemed a little subdued. A faint cool mist hovered around him, almost like a dark shadow which had begun to wrap itself around his weary shoulders. Ash closed his tearful eyes to rest a little and began to drift into a dream of days gone by.

At the age of ten – as one of the younger members of the imp clan, Ash had a sense of fun about him. His extended family had grown to love his cheeky nature and appreciate his inquisitive mind. As he grew, his family appreciated the qualities his curiosity would bring, as he searched for fresh knowledge to enhance the natural world around him. Being curious was a good thing, although it could also, at times, get him into troublesome situations. Generally, Ash had a co-operative and easy-going personality, although his siblings would say he was always a little mischievous. Having a special rapport with water, he loved the glade's stream which he used as his playground. More importantly though, he understood the water's true healing powers.

The desire to nurture was innate in every individual. Each Fidget contributed their own special gift to the cause, while their name was earned many generations before; they played it out through fretting and bustling about in their everyday lives. Ash was no exception, known famously for his fiddling ability, particularly when on important tasks.

With a strong sense of responsibility and a passion for caring for his environment, Ash tried constantly to support the vulnerable planet, albeit, in his small part; in his small world. He felt a connection with every wondrous, magical cell he helped. With a soothing voice, he could revive and nurture the wondrous plants, even those which seemed dead. He felt so proud of his charmed contribution to the Fidget's secretive way of life.

With sparkling blue eyes and a small misshapen nose, Ash was sparky and impatient. His dimpled, pale cheeks and rough, pointy ears were obscured slightly behind a head of delicate, yet wiry silver hair. His spindly arms were surprisingly strong as were his long, bony legs. Hanging from a string belt around his skinny waist, was his small scruffy, intriguing leather bag.

In flight, Ash remained quick – very quick. With unexpectedly large wings for the size of his body, when on the ground, they hid behind protective folds along his spindly arms. Each beautiful, delicate wing displayed discrete green and purple hues with fragile ragged edges.

Still in a dream, Ash thought about his brothers and sisters and the fun he once had zipping through the air around them. He recalled the fun times when he hid from his brothers and as he thought of his siblings, he wished he could compete with them once more, and enjoy each unique talent in their animated games. Ash loved that he could use his inner vision to transport himself to wherever he chose. All he had to do was close his eyelids and with concentration and a spot of imp magic, he could zip from place to place unnoticed.

Feeling exhausted, Ash dreamt of his special power and wondered if it would still work. He tried desperately to transport himself back to his family, but it seemed no matter how hard he tried he remained seated on the flat stone beside the dull stream, all alone.

It appeared that his unique power had gone. Feeling scared and alone, he wondered if his sudden, traumatic separation from his family had resulted in the loss of his skill. Trying to remain positive, he thought, 'Maybe, just maybe, after a rest, it might be OK.'

Ash placed his feet into the flow of the stream and swished them about a little. Looking through a blurry tear, he thought about the wonderful feeling he'd had when he was safe and secure. But now, everything had changed. He felt desperately alone and with the daylight fading fast, this previously animated imp sat alone and intensely frightened as he wondered what to do.

Ash needed to remain calm and focused on the minutes ahead as the dark woodland began to encroach all around him. A cold shiver went through his whole bony body, while another tear ran down his withdrawn, dimpled face and a long drip fell from his chin, splashing onto his bony knee. The diminished daylight made way for the thickening grey, cold sky and as a faint, cool mist covered the tiny imp, he lowered his head to think.

Without warning, a waft of air swished past him which left a faint trail of glittering light. This light gradually faded as it showered to the ground. Almost immediately, again, another swish flew past his other shoulder and glittering light again fell elegantly to the ground. Knowing his world so well, Ash was unsure and unfamiliar with this new life form. He watched with trepidation and fear as the glittering lights dispersed. Another waft of forceful air passed beside him and this time the light seemed more intense. He continued to watch the fading sparkles as they slowly showered down to the ground. Then, sitting beside the water's edge was a tiny butterfly, the size of a human thumb. Upon first glance it looked like a bright green leaf. But on closer inspection the tiny wings glowed with silvery shimmers. As Ash looked down at the tiny insect it spoke in a gentle feminine voice.

'My name is Sariel. I am the Fidget guardian angel and I am here to guide you.'

Ash looked through his sore eyes and could sense kindness and hope in this little insect. 'My family are gone. What has happened here?'

'Yes, your family are gone,' Sariel replied. 'I attempted to rescue you all, but at the last second you dropped from my shimmering shield and unfortunately were left behind.'

Ash looked utterly drained and with a breath of desperation, blurted out, 'Left behind? Where were you taking us? Where are my family now?'

Sariel sighed and sprinkled a canopy of twinkling light, this seemed to calm Ash a little, 'Do not fear as your family are safe and well. I transported them to another realm using the sacred Newid charm. I am afraid that you and your family were under direct attack from the beastly Brog. He had broken through your protective charm encircling your central glade. You must know your family cannot ever return and I am here to help guide you in finding a way to rejoin them.'

Trying to take in the words, thoughts rushed through Ash's muddled head, *'Will I ever see my family again? How will I find the strength to do this?'*

But as he tried to speak the words, he knew there was no choice. Giving up was not an option. He *had* to succeed, if he was to ever see his family again.

'You need to rest. I will protect you until the morning when we can talk once more. Please, close your eyes and sleep,' Sariel urged the exhausted creature.

Completely shattered, Ash grasped at a nearby log to lie his weary head upon and covered himself as best he could with some loosened moss. As the night drew in, he closed his eyes and gradually drifted to sleep.

CHAPTER TWO

Tilly the Explorer

Not too far away stood a row of ancient cottages traditionally made of rubble and stone, and occasionally of a mixture of earth and straw, the cottages were first built in the 19th century. Made by the people who lived in them and others at the time, the local mining community would share their knowledge of how a house should be. Now, in the latter part of the 20th century, if the cottages could talk, they would speak out for their proud ancient roots; and tell of the hardworking miners who once inhabited them.

In one of these interesting and quirky cottages sat Tilly. Tilly liked her own space and could be described as a loner. Spending most of her time enjoying the outdoor life, she often displayed a tomboy image, enjoying den-making and climbing trees. Comfortable in jeans and old trainers, she much preferred an untidy head of hair to a neatly groomed look. Though she had a scruffy appearance, for a 12-year-old girl, she knew exactly what motivated her. With extremely passionate views for saving wildlife, Tilly held a secret dream; to somehow make a difference to the world around her. She felt sure, that one day she could.

At school, Tilly appeared a little peculiar, a bit of an outsider, not part of the usual crowd. Being slightly introvert and shy, she found it hard to make new friends. In class, she did her best to remain attentive, although would occasionally daydream – something which was always mentioned in her annual school report. Her passion for nurturing living organisms and anything to do with nature, made her enjoy science lessons, particularly plant botany and human biology. Even at her young age, Tilly respected and appreciated all lifeforms being part of a complex holistic network. Her belief in helping to protect every living thing led to her being defiant in a science lesson one day, when she completely refused to dissect an earthworm. A science lesson not to be forgotten. She remained unperturbed however, with a determined passion and belief for all living things and their necessary contributions to the living world.

Occasionally, the school days held her interest, but most of the time, Tilly looked forward to the summer holidays, where she could explore the great outdoors with Grandad or learn new practical skills with her dad – perhaps learning to use a drill, or the practicalities of home decorating.

Being a Scorpio, Tilly's personality traits of determination with a good work ethic seemed to be very evident. At 12 years of age she had two older sisters, whom she found very annoying. The least amount of time she could spend near them the better. Her mum enjoyed anything equine and her dad owned a small boat, which he took on his latest big adventure out at sea.

Tilly's family home, in the countryside and near interesting woodlands, fed her curious nature and desire for learning and she would happily spend hours in the great outdoors. Her desire for outside learning was nurtured even more with a trip to stay with Grandad every summer, only this year it was not to be.

On this day, in Grandad's cottage, Tilly lent on her small, iron-framed bed and stared intensely at a cobweb in the corner of her room. She gazed in awe at the complexities of the design of the web and secretly admired the spider's talent that created it. Lying alongside her arm, Tilly's latest reading book *Stig of the Dump* was open at the page she had just read. She could relate to this story, as close to her family home stood an old disused quarry. When the mood took her, she would carefully explore the periphery, climbing its rocks and searching for bugs and she always imagined she might find her own friendly Stig one day.

It was nightfall and after a typical day with Grandad, Tilly usually assigned the evening hours to research and record her findings from the closing day. Only when she had evidenced the samples gained, would she go to sleep for the night.

Previously, every summer, Tilly and the whole family would travel to the quaint valleys to spend a couple of weeks with their elderly grandad, who had lived there all of his life. This year however, was different, very different. Tilly's family had gone to visit the cottage, not for a holiday, but to begin to sort Grandad's belongings.

To Tilly, her grandad was affectionately known as Teddy, the nature scientist. She was very close to Teddy and she missed him terribly. As an intelligent and very gentle man, he had a fascination for nature. Very unassuming, he had lived a solitary existence in the rundown cottage, yet was happy and settled there. His father before him spent life as a coal miner and worked in the nearby mining shaft for a living.

Over the years, during her visits, Teddy would sit with her and tell stories of his incredible adventures. Tilly always felt he had a vivid imagination and his stories would have her hanging on every word and urging him to carry on. Enthralled by his imagination and his intense stories, he brought excitement and adventure to every summer holiday. Tilly knew the stories were not real, but she relished them anyway, as she so admired her grandad.

Sometimes, during her stay, Teddy would return with unusual samples, gathered from the forest floor and needing further investigation under his special microscope. Tilly loved to get involved and magnify the samples on the little slides. She found it fascinating to see how the organisms looked at a cellular level. And she felt sure it was for these reasons she had always had such a driving enthusiasm for the natural world around her.

Grandad Teddy was nearly eighty when Tilly saw him last. The joints of his hands had become rather knobbly with extreme use over the years and his wrinkled face showed the ravages of time spent in outdoor exploration. Yet, he was still very much young at heart, relishing Tilly's company at every moment to share his stories and findings. They both shared a natural enthusiasm for the next big discovery and were so compatible in that way.

In each other's company, Teddy loved to listen to Tilly's boundless enthusiasm for nature; she could be her usual particularly inquisitive self and he would never tire of the conversation. She really missed him chuckling at her questions and would always respond saying, 'Don't worry, my tickling bees will know that.'

He would cup his hands together in a ball and pretend he had tickling bees within them. He'd say, 'Don't let them out or they'll tickle you,' and Tilly would have great delight in gradually pulling his fingers apart, against resistance, until the 'tickling bees' had been released onto a laughing and giggling young girl. They always had so much fun with those 'tickling bees.'

This year seemed so strange. Tilly spent hour after hour in quiet solitude. To fill her time, she would rummage around in the small cluttered garden watching, investigating and exploring. Every avenue of discovery would be pursued to include every small crack in every pathway. She was so keen to emulate her grandad, collecting samples to continue his cause; she really longed for and missed his expert eye.

Spending time alone in the small bedroom, Tilly had become familiar with the squeaky floorboards and the fascinating cracks in the walls. Yet, before Teddy passed away, he'd introduced her to

Whispering Wood. The intrepid pair would equip themselves with magnifying glasses, little glass pots, scoops and trowels. They would venture out together to collect specimens from the woodland floor. Tilly felt like a scientist herself as she observed his behaviour and copied his actions, mimicking him as he used his binoculars, which he never allowed her to use. She always looked forward to spotting something new and dreamt of finding a different, undiscovered lifeform, as in the stories Grandad would tell, but it never happened.

Tilly only ever entered the woodland in Grandad's company. Its density and undulating landscape created an eerie feel, particularly on damp days. Today was one of those damp, eerie days. Many years before, she had overheard her parents talking of rumours of Whispering Wood. While staying at the cottage, they had heard from some local folk that the woods were to be avoided. Some valley residents talked of ghostly misty lakes while others talked of unknown voices coming out of the trees, preventing anyone from entering.

Tilly's mum of course knew Grandad, her dad, had used the woodland for research and of course, with his experience she knew he would always keep Tilly safe on their small expeditions. Mum didn't really think the local rumours were true and she didn't believe in ghosts or that sort of thing.

This year, Tilly's family had come to the cottage during the autumn half-term. The nights were drawing in and the family had spent a couple of days already, gradually beginning to sort Grandad's things. On the third evening, while lying in bed, Tilly thought about her time spent in the garden. She concluded she had nearly exhausted every inch of the small cottage grounds in her thirst for exploring the natural world. While her parents continued to sort out boxes of belongings and deciding what to do with particular pieces of furniture, Tilly needed something new to focus her mind on.

The next day she awoke with no plan in mind. Normally she would know exactly what she planned to do, but after already having examined every speck of the garden, on this new day, Tilly just wasn't sure.

After breakfast she left the warmth of the cottage. Feeling a little chilly and aimless in the autumn breeze, she approached the rickety back gate at the end of the familiar back garden. Leaning on the damp, top rail and gazing into the daunting wood, the rising sun began to peer through the spindly pine trees ahead of her. Tilly recollected walking hand in hand with Grandad up a stony track and stretching her arms around an old oak tree to connect with its natural power.

Taking in a deep breath, Tilly sighed. Now her experienced and fearless grandad was no longer here. She wondered whether she might be plucky enough to venture into the mysterious wood ever again. Her mind seemed to dwell on this thought and she considered whether she could be brave enough to enter the woods on her own. Looking behind, with the cottage staring back at her, she wondered if she would be missed. As they were pretty much adults at the ages of 17 and 18, her annoying sisters had left early on a shopping trip for the day, so they weren't around to notice. Tilly thought of her parents, who were busy sorting things in the house. Even though she felt extremely enthusiastic for adventure, she felt they might not be too happy if she ventured out there all alone.

A moment of wavering bought Tilly back to reality as she remembered the special photograph she carried in her 'explorer' waistcoat pocket. After reaching for it, she took a moment to pause. The photograph showed her grandad kneeling in a lush, green glade. She did not recognise where the photograph had been taken but, in the picture, he wore his familiar woollen hat, a brown trilby hat with an unusual indigo feather in the surrounding grey band. In his stories, Teddy always said he did not remember where the feather had come from. The photograph also showed him holding his leather-bound binoculars, which he was never without on their woodland expeditions. As a young girl, with inspiring ideas, Tilly reminisced mimicking them alongside him, as she imagined herself to be as great an explorer as he was one day. With all the sorting out going on within the cottage, she wondered whether the binoculars might be found, as she desperately hoped to see them again. Staring at the photograph she noticed, in the forefront, a small tube of something. The photograph was beginning to show its age with worn parts around the edges and some of the image was a little smudged, obscured somehow, yet Tilly could just about see other small animals in the background which, at this moment, she took little notice of.

Still leaning on the gate, Tilly briefly closed her eyes to think. She then refocused on the sentimental picture and wished she knew a bit more about it. She was especially curious about the tube-like thing, but she felt it must be something to do with collecting specimens or a piece of equipment for preserving nature in some way.

Putting the precious photograph back into her waistcoat pocket, Tilly felt a renewed connection to Grandad with their shared love of nature and the complexities it presented. She missed him so much. All at once, she decided to be spontaneous. She reckoned that her parents wouldn't notice anyway, as they were so busy with sorting out Teddy's old belongings. And they were so used to her being a loner with her exploratory work in her room that they wouldn't suspect anything else. She slowly pushed the squeaky, mossy gate open and cautiously stepped out, towards the mysterious wood ...

CHAPTER THREE

The Protective Charm

Back at the central glade, Ash began to stir from his broken sleep. The morning mist floated just above him while birds emerged once more to chirp their collective morning song from the canopy of branches waving gently nearby. Awaking slightly dazed, Ash struggled to piece together the awful trauma from the day before. He wished it could all just be a terrible nightmare, but as he slowly looked around, feeling emotionally drained, the sight before him confirmed it as so *very* real.

With overwhelming weakness, and a sense of urgency, Ash needed to replenish some energy for the task ahead. At that moment, he wasn't quite sure what the task ahead was, but he knew he must keep going. With thoughts of his family, his inner determination urged him on. Immediately, his empty stomach and feelings of hunger motivated his next move so he made his way towards the damaged family tree, the ancient oak. It looked so sad, with drooping grey branches and lifeless bark, contrasting to when flamboyant, busy bugs bustled around its rambling roots. Staring at the dislodged turf, Ash cautiously checked for danger. He felt so insecure and alone as he knew, with the protective charm gone; the secretive glade could offer no protection from a potential menagerie of menacing, threatening beasts.

Embarking on unsteady ground, Ash clambered across uneven earth and past a cluster of damaged fungi to enter a small hollow, near the base of the tree. In the past, just within the tree itself, the Fidgets had created a pathway leading deep beneath the roots, to reach their clusters of harvested forages. Ash observed the recent destruction had torn the pathway completely in several places making his intended journey perilous. With very little evidence of the previously neat path, very soon, Ash lost his sense of direction. As he pushed on, sticky moments tested his resolve. He slipped and slid on the muddy surface, while his bony feet continually searched for the next safe step. Eventually, through the darkened route, he arrived and his stunned eyes met the store area for the first time since the devastation. It was completely transformed. Surrounded by cold, damp silence, Ash couldn't fathom the level of destruction and with roots hanging limply much of the food store had already gone. Sariel's description of the Brog being beastly was right.

The Brog, villain of the woodland, existed as a hog-like creature appearing fearless and mighty in nature. An elusive animal, with ownership of a long, blunt snout and impressive tusks capable of mass destruction, could rip through grass as easily as a child ripping tissue paper. Historically, the Fidget's biggest threat to their way of life was the Brog. Ash just knew, with the charm broken, it would not have been long before the beast laid claim to his free food feast.

In the damp, darkened space, Ash scrambled around to find anything fit for consumption. He desperately needed some nutrition to carry on. After a while, he discovered some bulging seed pods, known as puff seeds scattered across the muddy floor. These pods were fleshy and full of protein and without haste he scooped a handful to eat. They could also be eaten throughout the winter months, which was why they were a firm favourite with the Fidget clan. After eating the handful, hardly giving his stomach time to digest, Ash gathered further reserves and placed them into his small, leather pouch that hung from a tatty, yet surprisingly strong, piece of string surrounding his tiny waist.

Beginning to feel slighter better, he made his way back along the treacherous climb and out into the woodland air. Although, alone with his thoughts, he sensed encouragement from his absent family as he considered what to do next. In that moment, as if the little butterfly could read his mind, the glittering light appeared once more. Sariel landed close by and began to speak, 'I need to guide you. You have a long task ahead. Firstly, you must repair the protective charm for your glade once more. You will not be able to piece together what is needed for the Newid transportation charm, unless you have a place of safety to return to.'

Ash remained silent for a moment, allowing the information to sink in. To reinstall the protective charm, he knew he had to search for a specific tree, namely the ember tree; the intriguing tree which produced the magical fungus, but he had no clue as to where it was. Thinking quickly, he asked Sariel, 'Where do I find the special tree?'

But, as he looked towards his guide, a waft of air sped past and his guardian angel had gone once more. Ash thought about the protective charm which he had always known to be in place surrounding the Fidget's world. It must have been created so long ago and he never needed to even think about how it got there, until now. The charm, residing as a transparent shield, prevented any Brog from the wider woodlands from entering the central glade. As yesterday's events had shown, this charm was not, however, completely safe. During a full moon, it became possible for the unruly Brog to eat the charmed fungus. Normally, it would be inedible to him and any other creature, but at a full moon the fungus lost its bitter taste and the animal knew this. On any normal day, the fungus had an additional defence mechanism and could repair and reproduce itself within hours to secure the charm once more. Only, this time, at the latest attack, the fungus was no match for it and things were now very different.

With morning mists floating delicately by, many hours of daylight lay ahead. Ash was well aware of his need to create the magical circle using some special fungus from the mystical ember tree. He knew the tree disguised itself as a woodland beech and that it remained hidden among many trees which shared their space with the central glade. He also knew that when touched by an imp, the mystical ingredient would emerge from the base of the magical tree. The problem was Ash had no idea where to look, other than the periphery of the glade itself. All he knew was he needed to gather some tall, yet knobbly fungus to repair the protection and this was the prize for the desperately searching imp.

Looking out around the dense woodland, Ash wondered why Sariel had not helped him and he also deliberated over the length of time it might take to find the unique tree, if at all he was successful. But he knew one thing; he had to try, as it was vital for his future protection. It was now he urgently needed and wanted his special transportation power once more. Pausing to think, he thought, 'If I can use it to rejoin my family, then I won't need to find the ember tree or search for the Newid charm, will I?'

Ash considered his efforts the previous day, dealing with his trauma and shock. He reflected upon his attempt to rejoin his family then, as he remembered trying his special power without success. Now, in this moment, he thought, 'I've had a rest and eaten some food, I wonder?'

He closed his eyes tightly and thought of his family once more. With focused intensity and deep in thought, the seconds passed before he gradually opened his eyes. But Ash already knew, his inner vision had not returned. He lowered his head in despair. His unique special power had gone. His failure set off a chain reaction in his fidgety mind and panic set in as he wondered whether he could still fly at all. All imps could fly regardless of their special power and Ash in particular, was very quick.

With his small nose, he smelt the musky atmosphere around him. The air felt calm and, despite there being a damp aura, he gradually unfolded his considerable wings from their protective folds. His pumping heart filled with nervous excitement as he outstretched each large and delicate wing ready for flight and began to co-ordinate both beauties in unison. The increased momentum caused ripple effects along the carpeted ground, swishing loose leaves into the air. Without hesitation, with feet lifting from the ground, Ash's bony little frame shot up. Success!

A smudge of optimism had finally arrived. The relief Ash felt was immeasurable. For the first time, he sensed he might be able to complete this important step towards safety. With a methodical approach he began to fly rapidly from tree to tree, swooping towards each trunk and touching each one with his bony fingers. After each touch, he paused to stare at the base with expectancy, lingering just for a few seconds to see if he had found the *one* tree he needed.

Very soon, the minutes turned into an hour, then another and another. There were so many trees. It took every ounce of Ash's concentration to keep from missing a tree. There was no clue which cluster of trees had the necessary fungus he so badly needed. He began to tire and as he rested for a moment on the edge of the glade, he leant his weary head back on the base of a tree to look around. He was sure he had covered most of the encircled glade. There were just a couple of clusters of beech trees left. One of the clusters was in a dipped area and seemed to be on the darkest edge of the glade, with only partial sun reaching through the dense grove. Ash decided, after his rest, it would be these he would try next. Rubbing a small bead of sweat from his brow, he stroked his wings gently as if to encourage them to keep going.

Taking flight again, Ash soaked up the beauty and diversity of the woods below him. In flight, he usually felt comfortable to leave the safety of the glade, albeit just being a short distance away, but that quickly changed to immense fear each time he reached the ground. The tiny creature knew he could potentially bump into any threat at any time in the unfamiliar larger surroundings.

Reaching his target, he swooped down bravely and with an increased expectation, he touched the first tree, then the second and then the third ... the hope increased and then dissolved with every tree. But, just as hope began to fade once more, Ash sensed something happening. He could feel some movement. His expectant eyes opened wide and stared at the base of the tree. 'Could this be the ember tree?' he thought. He could hardly wait.

Delicate yellow spirals peeked through the undergrowth. Ash had never seen anything like it and he frantically collected each spiral as it appeared from the ground. He rapidly placed each piece into his foraging bag (with its own unique characteristic of being able to carry an unspecified amount without getting full). Ash tried to remain calm. He had a job to do. And he knew he had to stay focused to be able to implement the protective charm before the sun went down. With all the fungus picked and packed, he outstretched his paper-thin wings and intensified his flying speed back to his unprotected glade.

Back on the ground, Ash surveyed the torn land and looked to see where the previous protecting charm had been. He needed to get this right to ensure a tight circle be formed once more. He immediately got to work. He hurriedly, yet carefully replaced every single damaged fungus around the circle until it was all complete. Once placed in the ground, the odd spirals grew and grew until they stood quite tall. Relatively tall compared to a six-inch imp that is. Magically, the spirally fungus then began to expand sideways to produce a spirally broad stem with a yellow cup-like lid. The cup-like lids of the fungus seemed to fuse together in a show of defiance to the outside world. As it did so, a thin sheen of protection emerged from the repaired ground to form a transparent dome over the central glade – a dome that only the imp realm could see.

Ash collapsed with relief on a patch of moss and with a long sigh, rested his worn hands on his knobbly knees. A sense of accomplishment hit the drained imp as he rested, outstretched on the edge of the glade. Having repaired the damaged gaps, he felt an overwhelming wave of tiredness. He moved towards the trickling stream and rubbed his exhausted feet. Staring down into the dark valley, through weepy eyes, he knew he was the only *one* lonely imp now to keep safe.

CHAPTER FOUR

The Rustic Hut

After taking her first tentative steps along the stony track, Tilly stopped and looked back towards the cottage. She wondered if she should carry on. She thought of the all the special times she had spent with Teddy at her side and her thoughts urged her to continue.

Taking elongated strides, Tilly encouraged herself on, attempting to ooze confidence as she took in the route around her. She imagined herself to be an explorer on a secret mission to discover a new species as she took in the smells and sights with each step. After a few minutes, the track beneath her feet became more and more dense with untidy ferns and entangled brambles which reinforced the rough edges. Tilly's thoughts turned to her grandad's father, whom, she assumed, would have trodden along the same path many decades before, to reach his mine and then to her grandad, who became familiar with these dark and un-nerving woods from a very young age.

Very soon, the stony track seemed to disappear into the shadows of tall woodland trees. Rows of dense pines stood like soldiers in lines, while grand mature oaks showed their majestic strength in clusters. Looking up, the darkness of the dense canopy seemed to loom heavily above Tilly's head. Getting nervous, she looked behind, but the cottage was now out of sight. Pushing on, Tilly tried in vain to remember the routes she had taken before with her grandad at her side but it all looked so different now.

Till then, the route seemed relatively easy with only the one track from the cottage gate, but now the main route had dispersed and as Tilly continued still further she found herself forced to a standstill. Up ahead, things looked problematic; with a steep upward path ahead of her, there were also indications of pathways on either side. The canopy of the trees cast huge shadows preventing the full light of the sun to radiate around. Although Tilly could just see clearly enough at least three options to consider, possibly more. She now wished she had paid more attention to the routes she had travelled before with her grandad at her side, but he could not help her now.

Surveying the choices, Tilly thought long and hard. She considered turning back, towards the safety of the cottage, but then remembered the dark caverns. She knew they couldn't be far from her current position, because she had been there many times with her grandad. She remembered he had helped her to take small samples of the external rock to magnify. In fact, she was so impressed with the flint samples she collected, that at the time, she asked him to drill a hole in one. This she now wore on a bootlace around her neck. She'd always had a fascination with different rocks and minerals they collected. What stories they could tell, if they spoke, about where they came from. Tilly was no quitter and facing the choices before her, she wanted to reach those caverns, to remember those special times.

Taking another glance ahead, Tilly didn't think she recognised the steep incline, so she chose the path to her left, in the hope it would lead to the caverns. Proceeding once more, the woodland seemed to intrude more and more and as Tilly walked, the leafy fingers on the trees swayed, scratching each other's branches. In the dim light, she had to concentrate hard, and although she watched every foot step, she didn't seem to notice the increased undergrowth which had gradually replaced the, now hidden, track.

The whole route had become extremely precarious. Tilly began to see weird-shaped branches, small pot holes and other complex plant life for her fresh steps to negotiate. Every step emphasised sounds of squelching and crunching on the uneven ground, coated with autumnal growth. As she travelled further and further from the sanctuary of the cottage, the surrounding wildlife sounds seemed to become more and more restrained. Prickly brambles crawled close by, entangling each other while attempting to dance around Tilly's old trainers.

By now, peering ahead of her, Tilly could only see dense growth all around, with little natural light. Once more, she turned around to establish where she had come from, but any sign of previous footprints was lost among the brambly, muddy route. For the first time, she felt a tinge of regret about leaving the safety of the family's temporary abode. She began to wrestle with her thoughts, 'What would I do if I can't find my way back?'

Tilly knew her parents didn't even know where she had gone. Numerous thoughts raced through her mind and realising she should have left a note to explain, she made the decision (if she got back safely), she would make that a priority next time.

Staring at the occasional shafts of sunlight piercing through the trees ahead, Tilly listened. The beautiful birdsong had subsided and in its place, she thought she could hear some people in the distance. Suddenly keeping very still, she strained her ears to gain some clarity, 'Good,' she thought, 'they can show me how to get back to the cottages in the valley.'

After a few more moments, the voices were no clearer, if anything they were diminishing. In panic, Tilly started to run to reach them. She could hardly make out what was being said and, however hard she tried to get closer, the voices seemed to be at the same distance away. Tilly ran, hoping and stomping over the knotted brambly bushes and ferns which had multiplied and had covered the ground like a thick carpet.

In the next instant, the woodland dipped away and losing her footing, she slid on her mud-covered bottom down into a steep ravine. At the bottom and pushing herself up from the damp ground, she could not see anything familiar. No sign of the cavern area she had hoped to reach. Strangely reassuringly though, the whispering voices were still there, but this time they were to the side of her. Brushing the mud from her bruised rear, Tilly turned and stepped towards the voices. 'Why can't I see anyone?' she called out, into the dark, cold ravine – frustrated.

With her heart pounding, Tilly had no choice but to keep going. Curiously the forest floor began to feel soft, like spongy moss and the unforgiving ground began to slope once more. Tilly's old trainers were no match for the slippery surface and with little fight she began to fall to the ground. As she fell, the soft spongy moss wrapped itself around her and a huge hole opened up for Tilly to slide in. With her eyes tightly closed she prayed she was in some sort of bizarre dream. 'Yes, that is it,' she thought, 'I'm dreaming of course.'

Tilly wished herself back to her cosy snug bed in Grandad's cottage, with the damp patches on the walls and the elaborate spider's web in the corner. She glided down and down. But then, suddenly, she stopped, landing in a heap. She listened, waiting and wondering what to do next. Slowly, in fearful anticipation, she opened her eyes, not knowing what might be before her. The voices had gone. Tilly was alone and in what looked like a dingy tunnel. 'What *was* going on?' she thought. 'This *must* be a dream; it can't be real.'

Sitting in a disorderly heap on the earthy surface of the tunnel, Tilly's ears picked up an unfamiliar scuffling sound. It didn't seem too close at first, but the unusual sort of scraping noise began to get louder and louder. Tilly's feelings of terror increased. Here she was in an incredibly strange place, listening to something unknown which appeared to be, undoubtedly getting closer and closer. Just then, the noise stopped. Tilly shuffled away a little from where the sound was coming from, on the far side of the dreary tunnel she now found herself in. It was virtually impossible to see anything; the tunnel was so dark, although Tilly's eyes had adjusted enough to see movement coming from the opposite tunnel wall.

In the next instant, the wall of the tunnel began to bulge and small crumbs of soil erupted, trickling to the ground. Almost hyperventilating, Tilly pushed herself back to the opposite side of the dark tunnel, as far away as she could possibly go. The opposite wall continued to crumble away until the bulge resembled a volcano about to erupt. She braced herself for whatever was about to emerge and as she did so, saw two pink paws and a pink nose appear through the crumbly soil. Squinting hard to see, she could just make out the nose twitching as it sniffed its new environment.

'It's such a relief to see you. We have been waiting for so long. Forgive me, let me introduce myself, I am known as Old Hooky in these parts.'

Tilly stared without a word as her disbelieving eyes focused on a small grey creature with velvety fur and a distinct pink pointy nose. Perched on the end of the twitching nose was a pair of proud, cylindrical glasses with circular, oversized lenses staring back. Very nervously, Tilly asked, 'Wh-what are you? And how can you talk to me?'

The response came immediately, with a polite and reassuring tone, 'I can see you are wary; you need not be. I am a mole and I live in this hole. You have entered the magical realm within Whispering Wood and for that reason, you can hear me. The harmony within the realm is out of balance and it needs your help. You need to carry on, we have faith that you can help and we trust you to succeed. It has been lovely to meet you, but I must go now so you can continue on your way. Thank you Tilly, for what you are about to do.'

Old Hooky then crawled backwards, somewhat elegantly, into the same hole from which he had emerged, leaving a pile of crumbly soil behind.

Tilly sat, bewildered, trying to process what had just happened. Such a strange event, she could not quite believe. *Did she really have a conversation with a 'posh speaking' mole?*

Tilly's eyes focused upon a shard of light in the distance. It was unclear what it was, but as she was not too keen on the dark or the tunnel anymore, she quickly approached it. The light seeped through the edge of a square door, which was strangely on the ceiling of the tunnel. There was nowhere to go other than through the mysterious square door.

Tilly found this the most daunting and terrifying part of the journey so far. What would she find on the other side? Thinking of the completely bonkers conversation she had just had with a woodland mole; she had convinced herself she'd awoken within some sort of strange dream. With cold, shivery fingers, she pushed the square door, just a fraction so she could peer through the gap above.

With her eyes adjusting to the lighter space, it looked like some sort of old room. Thankfully, light radiated in from a small window above, so without further hesitation, Tilly pushed the square door open further and using her forearms and elbows, pulled herself up through.

Making a quick assessment of the surroundings, Tilly assumed she had arrived in some kind of room. Maybe some sort of barn or garage, she couldn't decide at first. Her mind worked overtime. She couldn't fail to notice her heart still pounding in her chest. Her body, still in high-alert mode, felt chilled and Tilly had no idea how safe she actually was.

The room itself had a small window; metal framed and rusted in places (but vital to gain a view of the contents within) and had a distinct damp smell in the air. The gloomy room could be described as compact with numerous irregular shelves adorning the walls, some overloaded with various objects such as recognisable tins of paint. One of the walls held an old cork noticeboard pinned with pictures and small pieces of mouldy paper hanging precariously here and there.

Tilly glanced around in bewilderment and to her delight, spotted a door behind her. '*It's a door*!' she said.

She jumped up towards it. Rattling the handle furiously, it could not be opened. Towards the top of the door a small frosted window let in more light, but spiders and mildew took most of the view to the outside and Tilly, could not see through clearly. She rubbed her eyes in bewilderment and concluded the ramshackle door was locked from the outside. Feeling confused, she looked down at her muddy clothing and noticed one of her trouser legs had ripped slightly. She also felt her icy cold toes within her wet, squelchy trainers.

How *had* she ended up here? Propped against the side wall, Tilly noticed a small round log standing on its end. Feeling completely deflated, she sat on the log and cupped her face in her hands. 'What *was* going on? This is just too weird,' she thought.

A subtle scratching sound interrupted Tilly's thoughts. It came from the other side of the dreary and unfamiliar room. Alongside the derelict wall was an array of wooden pallets and dented boxes. Tilly's ears followed the scratching sound as it increased behind a mouldy cardboard box. Having grown up in old cottages, she could recognise the smell as damp spores in the air from the mould and, as she considered the scratching sound, the cardboard box moved, just slightly. A tiny mouse scurried across the room to exit through its hole at the bottom of the rustic door. Curious and unruffled by the sight of the mouse, Tilly carefully moved the cardboard box and another small brown mouse raced away, leaving a half-eaten hazelnut behind and tiny pieces of chewed cardboard scattered around like mouse confetti.

Needing answers, Tilly searched for anything that might give her clues as to her whereabouts. As if to help her cause, shards of light filtered in from a couple of small gaps in the old slate roof where the tiles had slipped a little. Looking at the old wooden floor, she could see mouldy, rotten patches where the elements had dripped in through the tile gaps and onto the floorboards below.

Tilly felt she was the only person in the world right now – completely alone in this strange, yet exciting place where she somehow felt a connection to something. *Why did this place seem familiar?* She knew she had never been here before, yet she somehow knew all about it.

In a flash of realisation Tilly suddenly knew she was within the old rustic hut, a familiar part of Grandad's stories. She had never seen it before; in fact, she wasn't even sure if it was actually real. With Grandad's stories, you never really knew how much was reality and how much was fantasy. But here she sat on a wooden log within the much talked about rustic hut. This *was* reality; Tilly knew she was somehow there.

'This is incredible, this is awesome!' She jumped up from the log in excitement. 'Grandad's stories were epic … perhaps they were all real, no wait they can't have been. He talked about magical creatures and healing powers. But hang on, how did I get here? Surely that *was* magical? Maybe Grandad *was* a magician and this was his magical workshop? Maybe he called it the rustic hut, so I wouldn't suspect, Woo Hoo!' Tilly continued to ramble in excitement between giggling and taking a breath as she jumped and hopped around the uneven floor.

Without any thought about how or when she might return home, Tilly began to look around, more purposefully this time, full of excitement. Her inquisitive eyes focused on the cork noticeboard as she spotted an old photograph pinned to the cork. Removing it from the board, she looked more closely. There was Grandad in the picture and she could see from the shelving behind he must have taken the photograph of himself with his arms outstretched while working in the hut. 'How resourceful he was, not having anyone else there to take the photograph for him,' she thought.

Staring more closely, the photograph also showed an unusual butterfly. Tilly scrutinised the little insect sitting beside Grandad's microscope. At first glance it looked like a leaf with its bright green wings, but Tilly could just about make out two antennae so she assumed it was a butterfly.

There was so much to take in. Still glancing at the image, she studied the microscope, where it had been previously placed upon the work bench and as she looked more closely, she could see it was the exact microscope her grandad had left to her when he died. Suddenly feeling overwhelmed with sadness, she placed the photograph into her waistcoat pocket to join the other precious photograph. 'Grandad,' she said out loud, 'I promise to keep your adventures, dreams and passions for the natural world alive. This hut is such a secret and magical place and I'll aim to keep it that way.'

And with that she cautiously opened the square hatch door to make her return journey home.

Tilly re-entered the damp, dark tunnel and suddenly felt a ton of anxiety on her petite shoulders. She recalled how she had slid down a huge hole from the forest floor to arrive in this strange other world, but had no idea how she could climb back. She reached the point where she had fallen into a disorganised bundle and surveyed the ceiling above.

There didn't seem to be any evidence of a hole, yet Tilly felt sure she was in the right place.

Scared and alone, Tilly began to cry. Without hesitation, a soft whispering could be heard and from the wall in front of her, soil steps began to appear. Tilly froze and wondered if she could cope with any more surprises, yet she knew she had to get home and the whispers seemed to encourage her to climb. So, taking a deep breath with a large portion of faith, she ventured into the unknown and initiated the ascent.

It wasn't too long before daylight appeared and she could smell fresh woodland air. A menagerie of bird song filled the air and Tilly felt a big relief.

A little while later and Tilly arrived at the squeaky back gate just as Mum proceeded to push the dustbin to the front of the house, ready for the next morning's collection. 'Hi Tilly my love, I thought you were in your room analysing your garden findings?'

'Er, um, I was, but I had to come out to tidy the pathway of my trowel and little pots,' Tilly replied hastily, pointing to her exploratory equipment left beside the back gate. 'Phew, that was quick thinking on my part,' she said under her breath.

As she walked towards the cottage, Tilly couldn't help but notice the blazing sunshine and wondered how that could be as, when in the woodland, she seemed to have been gone for hours. Surely it would be the middle of the afternoon by now, or even later? Needing clarification, she rolled her dirty sleeve up to look at the time. To her surprise she had only been away for an hour and a half. 'What *was* going on?' Tilly wondered.

Safely back in the kitchen and feeling thirsty, Tilly grabbed a large glass of fresh water to consume. After gulping it down, she kicked off her muddy trainers in the hall and ran upstairs. She jumped onto her squeaky-framed bed and lay down to stare at the familiar ceiling. Tilly could not fathom what had just happened. She closed her eyes puzzled and thought about the sequence of events from the moment she had left the sleepy cottage. She knew she hadn't dreamt the experience. She had tangible evidence right there with her – the photograph of her beloved grandad with his microscope. The same photograph Tilly had discovered hanging on the cork board in the rustic hut. And then there was the meeting with the mole, Old Hooky, in the mysterious tunnel. She knew, without any doubt she had been there and back. The mud and the ripped trousers confirmed that.

Pursuing an answer, Tilly remembered the whispering voices and gasped, 'It was like the voices were leading me there. I got lost and they helped me to get there, through a magical way, the hidden, disused pathways, the magical dark hole, the tunnel and the square hatch door! Of course, that's why the main door to the hut was locked from the outside … that hut can only be entered by that magical way.'

Trying to keep her excitement under control, Tilly juggled her thoughts around. *But what about the time it took?* Staring at her off-white ceiling, she thought hard and surmised that the time she had been away from the cottage was approximately the time it took to walk to and from the magical hole which had transported her into the tunnel under the hut. Still completely confused, Tilly decided to waste no more time on something she couldn't explain. She scrambled off her bed to grab her notebook, eager to plan the next trip back to the intriguing hut. In her excited state, she hurriedly scrawled her thoughts and plans before they got completely muddled. The writing looked like an erratic spider had strapped a pencil on each leg to write the words all at the same time, but she didn't mind about that, as long as she could read it later.

With almost every thought now scribed, Tilly analysed the meeting with the mole and what the mole had said, 'Thank you for what you are about to do.' Rather puzzled about those words, she took a moment to pause and considered all those exciting tales her grandad had once told. The more Tilly thought about them the more she felt they were *actually* real, in a magical realm, a realm she was keen to explore with every available minute.

CHAPTER FIVE

Inventory

It was still only lunchtime. Tilly helped herself to a large bowl of Mum's homemade soup, from the simmering saucepan on the Aga. When the family stayed at the cottage, they often had soup, particularly leek and potato which was always Grandad's favourite. Even though he was no longer there, it seemed Mum still liked to make it anyway and Tilly found it a comforting reminder of the earlier times. Wafts of delicious aroma filled the kitchen and, as Tilly consumed the tasty dish, she had many things going through her busy mind; from better preparation for her next excursion, to wondering what she might find.

Wiping the last bits of buttered bread around the edge of the bowl, to mop up the last delicious bits, she thought of the mystical voices in the wood. 'Maybe *that's* why the locals call it Whispering Wood!' she exclaimed excitedly, looking around to check that no one heard her. Putting the empty soup bowl on the draining board, she rummaged in the cupboard and found a few chocolate digestives left in a packet. She hastily put them into her waistcoat pocket before racing upstairs to her room. Grabbing her favourite backpack, she placed her notebook and water bottle inside. Tilly then transferred the chocolate biscuits from the safety of her pocket into the backpack.

'Now, I need a plan.' Tilly knew her parents accepted she would spend hours in the back garden, which, fortunately for her, had lots of intriguing areas to explore. 'I'll write them a note and place it on my pillow – an emergency note, just in case I haven't returned and need them to come and find me. To cover all areas, I'll tell them I'm going to explore the garden and get samples from the wood behind, before doing my research in my room.'

Tilly sat at her organised desk, made from the top of a small chest of drawers, in what was Grandad's spare bedroom and she carefully wrote the VIP note; the 'Very Im Portant' note. Her parents never entered her room, except as a last resort, and she figured if they did and they read the note, then at least they would know to look for her, firstly in the garden and then in the woods. Rereading the note, she paused and thought. She really didn't want to worry them, but at least if they were looking for her, then the note would guide them to where she might be. Placing the note on her pillow, Tilly supposed that would be fine.

Just before departing, she looked around, 'Oh I nearly forgot, I need some small pots for samples.' She leant down under her bed where she kept a tray containing small plastic pots and other investigative objects. Gathering a couple of pots and a pair of tweezers, she placed them in her bag ready to go. Tilly then ran down the stairs and as she did so she called out to her parents, 'Mum, Dad, where are you?'

A muffled voice came back. 'We are in here love,' Mum's voice came from upstairs but Tilly couldn't work out where. With the question 'Where?' on the tip of Tilly's tongue, Mum responded again, 'We are in the attic.'

From above what was Grandad's room, a small wooden hatch gave access to the cottage attic. With very little room, he seemed to have filled it with numerous boxes, occasional suitcases; a couple of old pictures and other things people generally store in their attic spaces, when there's no room anywhere else.

'Ah OK, I'm off to do some exploring in the garden, I've had my soup for lunch, thanks Mum,' Tilly said, trying to sound normal.

'That's OK. We'll be up here for a while yet. See you later,' Mum replied.

Tilly usually had free rein on her activities most of the time and knowing her parents were occupied reassured her with the implementation of her plan. She grabbed her muddy trainers and sat beside the back door to put them on. She thought about her imminent expedition with nervousness. So far, her plan was set. All Tilly had to do now was find her way back to the rustic hut successfully. With her heart beginning to pound, she felt slightly off-colour, but her mind was set. There seemed so much she didn't know about Grandad's adventures in the woods, and having experienced a taste of the magic, Tilly was itching to discover more.

Creeping back through the mossy gate, the journey began once more, along the uneven, stony track. Tilly walked with purpose, yet felt more unease this time. She waded past the swinging ferns and trampled on the sharp brambles, preventing them from digging into her legs once more. Glancing above, she recalled the tall trees and dense pines which reminded her of a row of soldiers standing proud.

The quirky natural junction soon appeared and Tilly felt relieved to recognise the different directions, taking the left track as she had before. With each careful step to avoid any injury, she negotiated the natural holes and grassy mounds along the route and as she did so, she listened. She had arrived at roughly the area where the voices had appeared before. Tilly strained her ears for, as she continued to walk, she felt sure the voices should already be guiding her. But, this time, the voices did not appear, there was no sign of any whisper encouraging Tilly on. All she could hear was birdsong with the sound of her own feet scrunching along the track.

Without warning, just like before, the ground suddenly dipped away and Tilly slid down into an enclosed ravine. She felt the dark and cold atmosphere surround her again as she anticipated the arrival of the spongy moss beneath her feet. Still listening intensely for any whispers, Tilly began to panic, as she could not see any movement from the ground. Dark confusion and worried thoughts began to engulf her. She believed she had taken the same pathway, yet the journey appeared different somehow. Tilly had expected the moss to have appeared by now followed by the mystical hole for her to slide down, but there were still no signs of anything magical about to occur. It wasn't far to the hut, of that Tilly was sure, but this time, not even the whispering voices were helping her. She crouched down to look more closely for any clues of the spongy moss and a spirally bramble caught her on the hand. 'Ow, that's not nice!' she shouted, almost as if the bramble could hear her, 'What am I to do now?'

Unsettled, Tilly stood up and looked around once more. Shrugging her shoulders with bewilderment, she spun herself around in full circle and strained her eyes to gain some clue from anywhere nearby.

With no obvious idea and still no voices, resting just a few feet away was a knobbly old oak branch, just waiting to be sat on. With her head hung low, Tilly trampled towards it and slumped down upon the damp surface. With eyes closed and a lowered head, she felt a complete failure. She couldn't understand what she had done wrong. She really didn't want to but it seemed her only option, was to return home.

Just as she felt all was lost, her tired ears picked up a faint sound. A familiar rumbling sound became clearer and as Tilly glanced up quickly, she saw just ahead, the woodland ground beginning to shake. She watched intensely as the ground gave way and a small hole began to emerge. It got larger and larger until she could see a step inside, going down into the earth.

'This must be it!' she exclaimed with anticipation. 'This must be the entrance into the tunnel.' But then she paused. Talking to herself she said aloud, 'I'm not sure, perhaps this is a trap.' With her feet frozen to the woodland floor, she considered what to do. Peering onto the top step she could see another step below it. Then, as if to encourage her once again, the sound of the whispering voices arose from the ground.

Tilly tentatively put her left foot upon the top step. As she did so, more steps emerged beneath and as she walked, one step at a time, more steps appeared. After a short time, Tilly had reached deep into the dark underground space. She carried on bravely, down and down until there were no more steps to take. Tilly had reached the dark mole tunnel once more. Getting to grips with her bearings, she looked ahead and a shard of seeping light lit up the end of the tunnel and Tilly knew she had almost made it. 'I'm nearly there. Grandad's rustic hut is just there!' she exclaimed, with an overwhelming sense of relief. As the square door lifted, the familiar rays of sunlight filled the muddy tunnel. With stretched arms at the ready, it wasn't long before she had hauled herself back up into the hut once again.

Almost immediately, Tilly set to with her contents-discovery investigation. Being organised, however, before beginning, she emptied her backpack, object by object: the water bottle, notebook, chocolate biscuits and sample pots, onto the, definitely leaning, slightly wonky workbench under the small, obscured window.

From the window, unbeknown to Tilly, it was possible to see the central glade, where the Fidget family lived, and as she arrived at the hut, Ash, the solitary, yet intriguing, imp sat contemplating what he needed to do next to survive.

***

It had been a little while since Ash had successfully replenished the protective charm. He could already appreciate the rejuvenating stream which had begun to sparkle once more with its natural healing powers. The hypnotic sparkly bubbles of green energy floated along in the animated flow, as the stream made its way across the glade. Ash rubbed his tender bony toes in the refreshing water and the aches and pains from yesterday's trauma began to disperse.

'If only the stream had the power to create the Newid charm,' Ash thought. He knew the charm had been put together by a gentle giant from the human world but he had no idea where the giant was now. Ash had grown up with the knowledge that the human was a special friend to the imps. Alas, Ash also knew that the charm itself had already been used by Sariel, which had left him separated from the rest of his Fidget family. More importantly, he knew of a scroll somewhere giving details of what was needed to create the same charm. But where was it? And where was Sariel when Ash needed her?

Feeling somewhat protected now, the anxious imp could not escape his feelings of loneliness. He wandered along the edge of the sparkling stream kicking the air aimlessly and thought about the absent scroll. Looking across to the rustic hut, he sensed movement from within. Puzzled, he hopped over towards the derelict hut. He sprang onto the rusted window ledge and peered inside. He gasped to see movement through the old, cracked pane. Confused and extremely wary, Ash stared intensely at whatever it was moving around and he wondered how this rotten old hut, which had been empty for years, was now occupied.

Inside, oblivious to her observer, Tilly moved around the hut to investigate further. Using her little notebook, she began to record what she could see: an old cardboard box chewed by a mouse, two wooden pallets, a plastic gallon bottle with a broken lid, a few plastic plant pots with dried up soil and plant seedlings, a tin of whitewash and a couple of paintbrushes ... there was lots more, but that was a start. There were several cardboard boxes of various sizes, one bulging with old blankets and under the mildewed window was a pair of very dusty wellies.

Standing beside the wellies, Tilly leaned close to the grubby window to peer through. Little did she know Ash, standing upon the precarious window ledge on the other side, stared directly back at her, through the mildew-encrusted pane. Using her fingers, Tilly attempted to rub some of the ingrained dirt and mould away, but with little success.

Ash remained transfixed on the figure inside, while Tilly's squinting eyes could just about see the central glade. She had no idea she had been staring right through a hugely excitable imp, as he stared back at her with delight.

As time went on, Ash studied the human's movements carefully. He speculated whether this human knew the gentle giant who used to help the imps many years before. Perhaps this person could help introduce him to the gentle giant who was needed so much now. Still searching for answers and with no sign of Sariel coming to help, Ash decided this person could be very useful to his cause.

To make contact, the little imp had to somehow get creative. Looking at the door of the hut, he saw a gap, perfect for him to squeeze through. It wasn't long before he had sneaked in and jumped up onto the wonky workbench under the window. By now, Tilly's head looked like it had almost been consumed by a large cardboard box on the other wall. She purposefully rummaged through what looked like a significant pile of dustsheets or blankets from within. A cloud of dust filled the air, with little bits of cloth popping out all over her shoulders as her arms kept dipping in and out of the box.

Ash spotted Tilly's water bottle and got to work with his visual charm:

A little imp just likes me,
Is very important for you to see,
I'm putting my trust and faith in you,
So we can share the work to do.

With a shimmer of light and the touch of Ash's fingers, Tilly's bottle glowed for a second before returning to its normal colour.

Tilly came up for air from under the dusty blankets and coughed, heading for the workbench.

She flipped the blue cap off the water bottle and took a long drink through the spout to clear her dusty throat. Putting the bottle back onto the bench, she fell backwards in shock at the sight before her, 'Whoa! What ... who ... WHO are you?'

Ash stood and watched her immediate response carefully for fear of scaring her. Tilly, now sitting on the floor and staring up at the tiny imp, rubbed her flabbergasted eyes and blinked. Her breathing had doubled in speed as she tried to comprehend what she was looking at. In her mind, she considered whether this was another bizarre dream, but her thoughts were quickly erased as the tiny imp spoke, 'It's OK,' said Ash, 'I am hoping you can help me. I'm looking for the gentle giant from the human world and I'm hoping you can lead me to him.'

Tilly rubbed her eyes again in disbelief. 'But who are you? What are you? Where did you come from?' She blinked again and once more tried to refocus on the odd creature standing directly in front of her.

'I am the last Fidget and I need a specific charm to rejoin my family. I'm only a young imp but as far as I know this hut had been derelict for years. The fact that you have managed to get here somehow, tells me you have a connection to the magical realm.' Ash smiled a warm smile and with his soothing voice asked tentatively, 'Will you help me?'

Tilly slowly closed her gawping mouth. She thought about her journey here and what might still be discovered. Looking at the smiling imp, something told her not to fear this little creature. 'I am not sure what I can do, but um, yes, I will do my best to help you,' she replied. 'But I'm sure I have no connection to your magical realm, and anyway what use am I if I can't even get out of this hut?'

With that Ash flew down and straight outside through the small gap beside the door. He flew towards a spiky blue flower with emerald green feather-like leaves. He gently picked one of the blue spikes from the delicate flower head and flew directly to the rusty padlock preventing the door from opening. With a small amount of poking and wiggling the fused padlock became free and dissolved into a shower of dust.

Peeking through a split in the door, Tilly gasped in awe. Moments later, after grabbing her water bottle, notebook and chocolate biscuits from the workbench and quickly cramming them into her backpack, she carefully pushed open the stiff, creaky door and, in wonderment, stepped into the fresh, uplifting open air.

Tilly now truly knew she hadn't been dreaming at all and she really *had* entered a magical realm.

CHAPTER SIX

Joining Forces

Looking straight ahead, Tilly's wide-opened eyes fixed upon the central glade from which Ash had come. Before today, she had no knowledge of the imp's magical realm or even of his existence, although in this moment, she recalled elements of Grandad's diverse stories which spoke of such creatures.

There was so much to absorb. The glade itself looked disorganised, shambolic, like it had been mauled in some way, yet Tilly could see some evidence of a tidier existence. Beneath the apparent upheaval, neater sections of small pathways appeared, with a few delicate plants and ferns still intact, waving their wispy branches in the cool breeze. As if to protect the glade itself, Tilly observed towering, ancient, gnarly trees appearing to touch the sky as they encircled the glade, huddled together like a gaggle of geese.

After a few seconds to absorb the scene, Tilly looked down to the watchful Ash, who was still scrutinising her every move and carefully observing her reactions. 'I need to talk to you; I *really* need your help,' Ash exclaimed, beckoning Tilly to follow with his bony finger, he took flight and headed for the central part of the uprooted glade.

With huge anticipation, Tilly tentatively followed. Entering the glade itself, little clusters of dense shrubs shared their space with a regimented line of bugs. Upon first glance, the shrubs did not seem out of the ordinary however, each stem had masses of miniature white flowers covered in tiny filaments, like a silky fur covering. Tilly's attention was caught not by the look but by the smell of the plant, as exquisite waves of aniseed, not dissimilar to liquorice, filled the air. The smell reminded her of the Sherbet Fountains she liked to eat with the liquorice dip. She leaned down to look more closely and as she did so, became distracted by strange little grey bugs. Each bug followed another in an orderly fashion and upon closer inspection each one looked like a bit of moving bark.

With greyish-brown bodies, each bug marched along, one after the other, holding tiny blobs of something red in their jaws. Tilly slid into a slight hypnotic state as she watched the unusual bugs go about their business on the mossy ground. Never in all her hours of explorations or sample collections had she ever seen the like of these unusual creatures. A sudden tap on her shoulder brought Tilly back to reality.

'Please come,' Ash prompted, fluttering around her head.

As Tilly refocused on the direction she should take, she felt enthralled in this new domain, where all of a sudden, she could see weird creatures and unknown plant species at every step. She knew she was still in the local woodland, not very far from her grandad's old cottage, yet she seemed to be in another world, an unfamiliar, new world.

As if in an instant, the air around her filled with bright bugs going about their tasks. Strange buzzing noises filled her ears, one a sort of popping sound, while another gentle humming. A flash of yellow went past and Tilly felt the cool air as it did. She turned quickly to see a bright mustard-coloured insect, possibly a moth with large triangular wings moving elegantly through the air. Then, another appeared and as they flew together she observed their long tails curling around in an elegant dance. Tilly's enthralled eyes followed the pair until one landed on a nearby rock; flickering its wings to show a vibrant pattern of piercing red eyes in the afternoon's sky. As she watched, she presumed, the pattern was to ward off its enemies. Amazingly, these delicate creatures did not fret in her company and, as she walked along, they continued on their way.

After a short walk, the unlikely pair reached the sparkling stream close to the top of the glade. Ash landed on a nearby rock and waited for Tilly to find a suitable place to sit, once she had stopped gawping at the sights and sounds around her.

'I need to tell you of my plight,' Ash said with a serious tone. And with the sound of the tranquil stream beside them, he began to explain how he awoke alone, from the trauma of the Brog attack and how the Newid charm would enable him to rejoin the rest of his family.

Ash spoke of a kind, gentle human who had, in the past, helped to protect his family's way of life and of his knowledge of the charm, which had now, alas been depleted. Tilly listened intensely, trying to take it all in. She couldn't quite believe what was happening to her and as she listened, she shook her head and refocused her eyes several times, just to check the little imp was still there. Ash lowered his pale face for a second. 'I need your help to make the transportation charm. Please. I must be reunited with my family, wherever they are.'

With the enormous realisation that the incredible place was real, Tilly attempted to reassure the desperate imp, but in all honesty, she wasn't exactly sure what she could say or do. 'I am new here. I don't know how I even got here! I want to help you, really I do, but I just don't know *how* I can help you.'

She didn't know why, but Tilly felt sad, very sad. Her words went against all her beliefs about helping to nurture and protect all creatures in this world. The temperature around them seemed to drop significantly. The tall trees surrounding the glade swayed gently as shards of daylight shone down on the upset pair.

In the cool breeze, Tilly and Ash looked at each other. Two completely different species from different worlds, yet somehow, with a similar drive for good. After a period of silence, they took on a sense of resignation as perhaps nothing could be done. As the silent seconds passed, Ash wiped a drip from his small, misshapen nose and stroked some misplaced strands of his wiry hair from his face. With an exasperated breath, he eventually replied,

'But I know, somehow, that you *can* help me. You would not have been able to enter this magical realm if it were not *you* that could help.'

Tilly looked back at the intriguing hut from where she had come. She then looked at the devastation around her caused by the Brog. Desperate to help the pitiful Ash she said, 'I want to help you; honestly I do, but how?'

Just then, a shimmer of glistening light fell to the ground, all around, like a light rain shower. 'What was that?' exclaimed Tilly.

Ash breathed a long sigh of relief and replied, 'We are not to give up yet, just wait a moment.'

Another shower of glistening light encircled the pair, as they sat waiting and Sariel the imp's guardian angel appeared.

'Tilly has been brought here because she can help you,' Sariel said to Ash. 'She has the knowledge to find the scroll. The necessary scroll will eventually lead you back to within the arms of your family.' Sariel spoke with authority and purpose.

With a perplexed look on her tired face, Tilly responded, 'The scroll? But I don't know about any scroll?'

Without offering any further advice, Sariel took flight and disappeared into the distance. As she left, a shower of glittering sparkles fell through the air, only this time they cascaded some words as they fell. Time seemed to freeze as Tilly read the sparkling words falling to the ground, 'Oh, but you do, my friend ...'

Completely baffled, Tilly looked at Ash and remarked, 'I must be the wrong person. I don't know about any scroll.' Exasperated, she raised her arms in the air with her palms showing as if to emphasise that she couldn't help.

'But you must,' Ash insisted almost instantaneously, 'creatures in the magical realm are never mistaken. Please think about what you know.'

Feeling puzzled and slightly useless, Tilly reached into her backpack for her drink and the chocolate biscuits. Her stomach was beginning to tell her it needed some sustenance, so she drank some water and consumed two of her favourite chocolate digestives. While doing so, she thought once more of what had happened since finding herself in the rustic hut. She needed to understand so much. It was like she had a giant jigsaw puzzle in her head and the pieces had all been jumbled up. Tilly found herself frantically trying to unscramble those pieces to put them back together in a logical order once again. She felt lost in her thoughts trying to fathom some answers, anything that could help the tiny imp's plight.

Tilly's head hurt. She kept thinking about what Sariel had said. The words 'she has the knowledge to find the scroll,' kept whirling around in her confused thoughts. Once again she imagined a giant tennis racket hitting these words away with, 'I don't know of any scroll.' But then, abruptly, she jumped up into the cooling air and exclaimed, 'Of course, the scroll! That's what the tube-like object is in my photograph. That's it! I knew about it all along!'

Tilly's shaking hand scrambled for the precious photograph tucked safely into her waistcoat pocket. Ash, waiting patiently for her to remember anything that might help, fell off his shiny rock beside the stream in excitement before rocketing closer to the photograph. The spirited pair then huddled together and stared closely at the picture. There was Grandad, kneeling on a lush glade, wearing his brown trilby-type hat with an indigo feather in the grey hat band. Looking at the lush grass, Tilly now knew he was in the central glade as it once was. And there it was. The object of such significance, the small tube, resting on the ground near Grandad's kneeling knee, the scroll itself! The old Polaroid photograph was clear proof that Tilly's grandad had been here and that he had formed a connection to the Fidget realm in this vital way.

Without haste, Tilly began to explain she was the gentle giant's granddaughter and that they used to spend a lot of time together gathering samples and sharing knowledge of the natural world.

'My family would see your grandad at work in the rustic hut and I have heard stories of my relatives spending time with him there,' Ash said, 'I am now alone though, so neither my family nor your grandad can help.'

Ash looked at the concern on Tilly's face. He wondered if she had a plan or even knew where to look for the vital scroll.

'It's all very well to have a photograph showing the object, but that's no good, if you don't know where to find it,' he said.

However, Tilly was Ash's only hope and he had to put his faith in her. 'I know you can help me now,' said Ash with a warm smile. 'I knew you were the one, when I saw you in the hut, that's why I sprinkled my visual charm into your water bottle. That is why you now have the power to see me and all the other wonderful life forms in this special realm.'

Tilly felt an overwhelming sense of responsibility. Teddy wasn't here anymore and couldn't help the distressed imp with his plight. But with every bone in her body, she felt she just might be able to. She owed it to her grandad and to the future generations of the Fidgets to see if she could do this. Without even considering the challenges that may lie ahead, Tilly knew she must, at least, try. She carefully considered her response before speaking. 'We will start with the hut. There are lots of boxes and most likely, other things obscured in there, which might hold the clues to the scroll's whereabouts. That is where we will start.'

As she looked towards the hut, the daylight seemed to diminish, and thinking about the uncertain journey home, Tilly checked her wrist watch. But how strange! It was only two-thirty in the afternoon. Time, seemed to have slowed right down. Slightly puzzled, yet weirdly accepting the manipulated time, Tilly stood up and exclaimed, 'OK, let's head for the hut. We will see what we can find before I head home.'

And with that, the like-minded pair from two different worlds set off on the short journey, from the protected glade to the mystical rustic hut, to begin their search.

CHAPTER SEVEN

The Missing Scroll

Ash led the way towards the ramshackle hut. Checking her backpack was still on board Tilly hopped down the small pathway behind him. As she did so, she couldn't fail to notice one of the delicate feathery ferns which lined the side of the pathway, unfolding in front of her. Tilly stopped abruptly to watch. As the fern fronds began to uncurl, so did a small blue flower head and to Tilly's amazement, it began to speak.

'Remember to remember you are part of the secret realm now and what you discover here; what you go through here, must always stay in your heart. There may be challenges ahead, but you must persevere, for the sake of the Fidget world and all that is part of it. Tilly, you are one of us now.'

Before Tilly had time to blink, the small blue flower had tucked itself away within the feathery fronds, as if nothing had occurred. Seconds passed and she rubbed her eyes in disbelief. She jogged towards Ash who was already nearing the entrance to the hut.

Standing facing the old wooden door, Tilly looked once more at where the padlock once was. How incredible it was she thought that a spike of a flower had caused it to dissolve. She imagined what it must be like to have such magical powers and contemplated the amazing sights and wondered what else she might see in this mystical land.

Thinking of the task ahead, Tilly wrenched open the rusty door and stepped inside. Old paint splintered off and Ash fluttered up onto the wonky workbench under the window.

'Now, where do we start?' she said.

Everything in the hut was in chaos. Cardboard boxes, plant pots, old plastic tubs, small trowels, sample pots, seed trays and other unrecognisable objects lay about the shelves, along the workbench and random places across the floor. As Tilly had seen before, on the wall, the fixed cork noticeboard looked in relatively good order, with a few bits of paper pinned to it, alongside magazine pictures and plant labels. Every object came dressed with an extremely dusty coat and with evidence of spider inhabitation. The sheltered, remote hut proved to be the ideal homestead for hordes of spiders and mice in permanent, cosy residences.

Deciding to start near the door and feeling very important, Tilly opened a damp cardboard box, amazingly still intact from the occupying mice. Lifting the flaps, she held her breath as a small dust cloud filled the air. Inside there were little pots of varying sizes. Some of the smaller ones were recognisable as the sample pots Grandad had used when collecting small pieces of unidentified flora. Following her investigation of the first chosen box, Tilly satisfied herself there was no sign of anything resembling a scroll. Then she placed the box in the corner of the back wall. In her organising mind, she had decided that area would be where the checked boxes could be placed for now.

Trying to continue in a methodical way, the pair searched through another cardboard box, but they discovered little other than more plant pots and a small bag of garden compost. Tilly stood up and slowly scanned the walls of the hut. With so much to go through, she felt she needed some clue of direction and as she looked her eyes met the corkboard once again, 'Maybe there is something on there to give us a clue?' she said to Ash.

Taking a few steps towards the board, the first thing that caught Tilly's eye was a picture of a plant which had been roughly torn from the page of a magazine. The picture showed a shrub of unusual shape and form. Tilly had not seen anything like it before. 'What is this strange curly plant?' she asked, as she turned to Ash.

But Ash had moved from her side and was now staring, motionless through the cloudy window up towards the glade. Hearing her words, he took flight and rested gently onto her hand to see, 'That's the Brog's food. It's what they eat, well mostly eat.'

'But I don't understand,' she replied, 'why did the Brog destroy your food store if they had other food to eat?'

Ash explained, 'The Brog's main food source is that plant.' He stared at the same image, 'It's the crimson tassel plant and it tends to grow on lower ground, near the caverns, so I've been told. I don't know why the Brog made the attack, but I was always aware that he could, as he also feeds on our puff seeds, the ones we store through the cooler months. That is why we always had the protective charm to help shield us from the danger.' Ash gasped, 'Of course! Recently, with all the storms, the Brog's plants could have been flooded and in short supply. That could be why he came searching for our seeds!'

Tilly looked carefully at the picture of the plant. It looked like a type of hazel tree, although compact and close to the ground. The branches grew in coil form, creating interesting architectural twists and spindles, like a collection of corkscrews twisted together. Hanging from the twisted branches the picture showed rods of delicate seeds, in vibrant crimson. Tilly hoped she might get to see one of these intriguing plants to enable her to take a sample, thinking it would make a perfect addition to her current research.

Looking for further clues, she continued to peruse the corkboard. A corner of another photograph could just about be seen peeping out from under an old plant label. Tilly liked pictures and with excitement she lifted the plant label. 'Hey, Ash, have a look at this!' She unpinned the previously obscured photo and took it hastily, to the light beside the window. The photograph showed Grandad's microscope and beside it on the workbench, not far from where Tilly was now, was a Fidget!

Tilly and Ash stared at one another, 'Who is that?' Ash shrieked. He had been told the gentle giant had met some of his kind, but he didn't know who. Straining his eyes, he tried without success to see who it was. The damp had affected the surface of the picture and it was impossible to distinguish any details. Stunned into silence, both Ash and Tilly continued to stare at the image.

Breaking the silence, a scurrying mouse shot across the floor, from under a pile of bulging blankets filling another cardboard box. Tilly placed the precious photograph on the workbench and remembered, earlier on, a coughing fit had stopped her rummaging through a pile of dusty blankets. It seemed as if the mouse was reminding her to continue to search. She was here to look for the scroll after all.

Tilly set to with the pile of blankets. She methodically lifted each one from its pile and transferred it to another pile in the corner of the back wall – where the organised area remained. After shifting a few blankets, the view into the box itself became much clearer. Tilly spied something made of dark wood, a proper wooden box of some kind. The next blanket unveiled a solid wooden chest, not huge, about the size of a large tool box. Resting on the top were a pair of old gardening gloves and she assumed the accompanying box was full of her grandad's gardening tools, so she placed it upon the workbench for later inspection. Her main focus was looking for the much needed scroll.

Feeling thirsty, Tilly sat down on the upturned log seat and grabbed a drink with biscuits to eat. She glanced out at the fading light and wondered what the time was, back home, at her grandad's cottage. It felt like a long time had passed since she last looked and she still felt extremely nervous in case she was missed. Cramming the third biscuit into her mouth, Tilly scanned for the time on her wrist watch once more. It still only said three-twenty, but feeling a little uneasy about it, she decided she couldn't stay much longer.

With her heart wanting to continue the search, Tilly opted to check one more container before heading home. Before she chose the last container, she got distracted by a sight. Just below the wonky workbench sat an old pair of wellington boots. The rims of which were coated in a layer of thick dust. Between each boot, from around the rim, a delicate cobweb hung like a trapeze from one rim to the other. With her fascination for spiders, Tilly searched for the inhabitant. She followed another trapeze line to a nearby plastic lidded container and just under the lid she made her discovery – the resident guest's cover had been blown. Carefully scooping the spider into her hands, Tilly removed it from the edge of the lid so she could open the container. She placed the spider safely down into the corner of the hut before returning to open the chosen container, 'This will be my last thing to search for today,' she announced.

Tilly opened the lid to reveal a mundane find inside, just a few measuring jugs, sample pots and storage dishes, used as part of botanical research. Uninspired, and beginning to need the safety of home, she stopped, 'OK, well, that's it for today, I will come back to continue the scroll search tomorrow, I promise.'

Ash held his hands together, as if to pray, and Tilly gathered her belongings in her faithful backpack ready to head home. Lifting the square hatch door to re-enter the tunnel, Tilly glanced at the casual plant pots on the hut floor. Next to them were a group of small pebbles. She found them intriguing and unusual. She retrieved one and slipped it into her backpack for the journey home. Then, without further delay, re-entered the dark tunnel, leaving Ash hoping she would return the next day.

CHAPTER EIGHT

The Discovery

The next morning, Tilly awoke sharply with the sound of clinking crockery meeting the old kitchen draining board below. The cluttering sounds continued as she pulled back the covers and rubbed her weary eyes. Tilly had had a restless night; the images of the previous day just whirled around her head, like clothes spinning in a washing machine. Sitting up, she grabbed her watch from the little cupboard beside the bed and to her astonishment it was nearly 8.30am. 'What, wait, I set my alarm for 7, what happened?' Checking the alarm, it was still set. With blurry eyes and very little energy, Tilly now appreciated how tired she actually was, after all the tossing and turning in the night.

After hurriedly getting dressed, she flew downstairs to have some breakfast. As she entered the kitchen, she was greeted by her mum who had just finished clearing the breakfast plates. 'Morning, Darling. We have to go into town this morning to visit your grandad's solicitor. Do you think you will be OK here on your own?'

Tilly's eyes widened as her mind worked overtime and she responded quickly, 'Yes, I'll be fine, thanks. I'll just continue with my explorations and research of my findings,' she replied, trying to sound scientific, while attempting to calmly fetch the sugar puffs from the cupboard.

Tilly began to speculate about her two annoying sisters when her mum said, 'The girls are coming too, we are dropping them off at the cinema and if you think you'll be OK, we might stop off for a bite to eat before we all return. Is that OK Tilly? Do you want to come with us?'

Mum was always in a rush, even speaking her words she had already focused upon leaving and had reached halfway towards the stairs, not really fully listening to Tilly's response.

Tilly was used to entertaining herself and quite liked her own company, she preferred it that way. 'It's fine, I'll stay here, don't worry about me.'

Taking large gulps from her cereal bowl, Tilly was excited. 'This is perfect,' she thought, 'I will have loads of time to continue my search and to help Ash in Whispering Wood.'

Ten minutes later, Mum and Dad were rounding up the older, giggling girls and everyone was about to leave. 'There is still a lot of stuff to sort through in the attic if you fancy it?' Mum said as she went through the front door towards the car.

'Bye Mum, see you later,' Tilly replied standing by the front door to wave them off. She very much wanted to make sure she had witnessed them actually leaving. The coast was clear! Running upstairs at full pelt, Tilly seized her essential backpack, which she had already prepared the night before. Looking out of her bedroom window, she made a final scan of the lane, both up and down, to check a final time that the coast was clear. In no time at all, with everything prepared, she made her way from the bedroom, quickly revisiting the kitchen to place a peanut butter sandwich and other chosen snacks into the backpack before heading towards the back door and into the garden.

Soon enough the magical journey through the captivating wood began once more. This time, Tilly felt more confident in the route and she quickly reached the spot where the magical hole had previously emerged. 'Yes!' she exclaimed as the underground steps miraculously appeared as before and soon enough Tilly found herself back inside the familiar and intriguing hut.

Finding the backpack a little heavy, Tilly removed it from her shoulders and placed it beside the hut door. As quickly as she could, she looked around for Ash, but to no avail. For some reason, she assumed her imp companion would be there waiting for her, but as it was, she felt sure he wouldn't be long, so she set to work.

Box after box Tilly searched, but with no sign of any scroll. After what seemed like an age and with Tilly sure she had searched every part of the hut, there was still no clue as to the whereabouts of the sought after scroll. Tired and frustrated, she rested on the rustic log. Tilly just didn't know what to do next. Not wanting to admit defeat, she pushed herself on. 'There must be something here,' she thought.

It was not in her nature to give up and thinking about her next move, Tilly scanned the four walls again. This time, on the floor, she noticed the group of dried-up saplings in their plastic pots once more, with the smooth pebbles beside. She recalled picking a pebble up the previous day and feeling inside her backpack, it was still there.

Leaving the pebble in the backpack and feeling a little peckish, Tilly reached for an oat bar from the side pocket and as she chewed her way through it, she stared up through the musky window above the workbench. As she did so a shower of sparkles rained down onto the workbench in front of her. 'Keep searching and you will find,' said Sariel calmly, as she appeared from the sparkles showering down, 'you need to keep on looking.' And then, as quick as she appeared, she had gone once more.

Tilly felt exasperated, 'But I've searched and searched.' Unfortunately, her voice just filled the empty space in front of her and the hut's knowledge of the scroll remained hidden through the quiet air all around. Tilly took the last bite from her nourishing bar, stood up and made her way to the cloudy window, hoping to see Ash this time. As she leant on the workbench, her elbow nudged the wooden tool box sitting on the top. Resigned to her feelings of disappointment, she tried to remain upbeat and thought it would be interesting to have a look at Grandad's gardening tools instead.

Grabbing the old metal clasp, the hinges squealed slightly as the lid of the box slowly opened. An old cobweb broke away from the corner of the box as Tilly glimpsed something brown. She lifted the lid even more as she wondered whether the brown object inside was a tool handle of some sort. But in an instant, the penny dropped ... it was Grandad's hat! The brown trilby hat he wore in the precious photograph, was sitting proudly in the box. With a racing pulse, she reached for the hat. Needing to blow another cobweb from the top, she turned the hat around and to her delight an indigo feather came into view. Tilly gasped with excitement, not quite believing that her grandad's hat in its full entirety had kept in such good condition in the old wooden box. 'Wow!' she said.

Tilly couldn't resist the temptation to put it on and just for a moment, placed the hat onto her small head, pushing the rim up from her forehead to prevent it from falling over her eyes. She dreamt of her wonderful explorer days spent with her heroic grandad. Then, after a minute or two, she carefully removed the hat and placed it on top of the bench.

Tilly took a couple of deep breaths as the anticipation of what else she might find increased, before peering into the box once again, she spotted a couple more photographs and looking at each image saw living saplings in pots, with curly branches. The plants seemed familiar, but with everything she had experienced in the last twenty-four hours, for a short moment, she couldn't place where she had seen them before. Suddenly she realised, 'Of course, it's the dried-up saplings as proper plants!' Each image also showed more of the strangely smooth pebbles, which she assumed Grandad used for decoration around each plant.

Before returning the photographs to the box, Tilly scanned through a collection of rope. The rope seemed very thick, relative to the size of Tilly's hands and some of the pieces had puzzling adjoining hooks on the ends which didn't interest her, so she continued looking. Underneath the bundles of rope she spotted an old rag which seemed to be wrapped around something. With increasing curiosity, she lifted the grey rag from the box. Resembling an old duster, Tilly unfolded the rag and a hard, brown leather case came into view. Attached to the case was a thin leather strap, with an additional strip of leather securing the lid of the case to the adjoining buckle. A broad smile reached across her face and although the case itself looked rather scuffed and scratched, its tatty appearance did little to dampen Tilly's enthusiasm for the object. Pulling the leather strip from its buckle, she opened the case and there inside was what she had hoped – Grandad's pair of binoculars. She couldn't believe it. What a day she was having! First she had found his hat and now, here in her hand, were his binoculars! Tilly lifted them from their case and remembered how Grandad was never without them. She reminisced with thoughts of accompanying him on his nature walks and recalled with fondness how protective he was of his binoculars, never allowing her to use them.

Not wanting to go against his wishes, even now, Tilly promptly placed the binoculars back into their case and then quite carefully into her backpack for safekeeping.

Returning the wooden box to continue her search, one last thing caught Tilly's eye, a nondescript wooden log tucked neatly into the corner of the box. It seemed a bit odd for a wooden log to be stored within a wooden box, but, she thought, it looked like a perfectly normal log, covered in rough bark, similar to her newly acquired 'sitting log' within the hut.

Tilly continued to dismiss her thought and with the full contents of the box explored, she picked up Grandad's hat from the workbench to return it to its home. As she did so, she glanced at the internal log once more. Something was poking out from its centre. Something nagged her to look more closely. Leaving the hat on the bench once more, she lifted the log from the box and placed it onto the workbench. It had been hollowed out and there within it appeared to be a roll of something. Taking care not to damage the object, Tilly gently grasped the corner of the mysterious roll. As she pulled, she couldn't believe her sight, a roll of paper began to emerge, definitely a roll of paper! Was it the scroll? With utter disbelief and almost forgetting to breathe, she pulled the whole roll of paper free from the centre of the log.

Tilly stared at the roll in front of her. The colour, not dissimilar to tea bag stains, a batik mix of pale browns, with patches of darker brown and slightly damp edges. Around the centre, a piece of twine secured the roll in place, tied loosely. Tilly knew this could be it. What else could it be? Glancing around, Tilly hoped her little friend had arrived, but Ash was still nowhere to be seen.

Before even thinking of opening it, affirmation was needed, so she reached into her waistcoat pocket for the treasured photograph. There it was, the photograph of Grandad kneeling onto the glade with the scroll beside his knee. Tilly quickly scanned the photograph and compared it to the roll of paper, to assess any similarities. She couldn't quite believe she might *actually* be looking at the scroll.

For a while, Tilly just stood and stared. Her mouth had gone dry as the anticipation filled the room and her heart leaped in excitement. Almost too nervous to open it, she wondered what on earth it would contain. Seeing the photograph and her beloved grandad again, Tilly appreciated even more his great passion to protect the Fidgets – such a vulnerable and magical species. For the sake of the Fidgets, Tilly knew she had to do all she could. They really needed her; her new friend Ash needed her. Tilly needed Ash right now. 'Where *was* he?' she thought.

It was vital Ash was present for this incredible moment. Tilly carefully picked the paper roll up and pushed open the rickety door. She headed for the imp's glade with new enthusiasm. As she walked, the whole forest came alive around her, as if each living thing had recognised the importance of her find. The air was thick with flying bugs and an array of peculiar noises filled Tilly's ears like a symphony. Holding the scroll tightly, she found Ash asleep beside the stream in his favourite spot. The same spot where he first explained his awful plight and where he initially asked for her help.

Ash opened his eyes and immediately flew into the air to greet his new friend. His delicate green and purple hues fluttered near Tilly's shoulders before settling onto her arm. 'Look, look! I've found the scroll!' Tilly exclaimed.

Ash flew up and twirled around in a celebratory dance in the air and exclaimed, 'YES, I knew you could do it, let's open it. Come on, quick!'

With the pair sat on a patch of soft grass, Tilly gently pulled at the scroll's twine bow to release it. As it released, the paper roll unfurled and she carefully grasped the edges to open it up. Slowly unrolling the scroll, the pair made eye contact, hardly believing this moment. As Tilly held her breath, some writing began to emerge bit by bit, as the scroll unfurled. With the roll completely unravelled, there was a lot to digest. Before saying a word, Tilly quickly surveyed what she saw – the first section presented a detailed paragraph. Then, there followed a sort of verse or poem. Lastly the scroll presented instructions numbered one to six. She tried to keep her composure as Ash tapped her on the shoulder repeatedly, so she began to read the whole piece, right from the top, slowly and clearly.

'To whom it may concern,' Tilly took a deep breath and continued, 'this scroll provides the reader with the necessary details to complete the Newid charm. If you achieve this, you will be helping to protect the future of the secretive and magical Fidget species. As the reader, you have already been welcomed into the mystical realm within Whispering Wood and you will be privileged to witness the most beautiful diversity this planet has to offer. You are now stepping into my former footsteps and I wish you well. You will need to read the following verse and instructions carefully to ensure success, yours mystically, Teddy.'

Tilly paused for a moment. She felt so very proud, but had absolutely no idea how complex her grandad really had been. It was clear Teddy was an integral part of the Fidget world and he had obviously spent many hours within the imp's realm helping to protect their way of life. Tilly continued reading:

This scroll will help you see,
The necessary things to make this be,
With all the ingredients that you find,
The recipe complete and can be bind.

The mystical hut can serve you well,
For other resources I cannot tell,
But keep in mind you must succeed,
And save the precious Fidget breed.

Have faith that this can be done,
For you've been chosen as the one,
Use your knowledge and your friends,
And keep the hope for a good end.

Tilly took a really deep breath and kept going, as Ash grasped one of her fingers held tightly along the edge of the scroll.

1. Gather a stalk of the deadly cap fungus. Use the bark bugs and the Arion bird to help you. Store safely until ready to use.
2. Collect a piece of discarded tusk from the Brog's cavern. Use the yarrow white flowers to give you sight. Store safely once again.
3. Add a sprinkle of sparkling water from the central glade.

4. Pick one strand of hair from the intrepid explorer undertaking this task ready to place into the mix.

Tilly took another calm breath and continued:

5. To create the charm itself, place the stalk of deadly cap fungus and the shredded tusk into a container. Add the sprinkle of sparkling water and be ready to add the final ingredient, the strand of hair. When the hair is added the charm will emerge ... ensure you catch it or all will be lost.
6. Finally, Sariel must be given the completed charm. It is only she who can implement the charm successfully.

The reading was complete. For Tilly, lowering the scroll to her knees, the reality of what was ahead hit home. Could it even be possible? She would need to use all her knowledge and more to achieve what was being asked of her. But if anything, there was no doubt she was determined. Growing up, it was ingrained in her as she learnt from her grandad, who taught long ago that determination and perseverance would often lead to success. Tilly knew, just accepting this challenge was the most important thing she could do to continue her grandad's work in preserving the Fidget world. She also knew, even though he wasn't here anymore, he would be urging his granddaughter on.

Ash couldn't contain himself. He jumped up and down in excitement, and true to his name, kept fiddling with his foraging bag keen to start collecting. Tilly smiled, thrilled to see the animated side of the impressionable imp. Until now his lively personality had remained hidden behind a shield of uncertainty and she absorbed every second of this new, excitable behaviour. Ash's whole persona had changed from a subdued, sad little creature to this bundle of energy springing around the mossy ground nearby.

Tilly tried to calm things a little with some direction, 'We need to plan this carefully. You have a think about what you might need and I'll go back to the hut to gather my thoughts.'

Ash, still bouncing around like a peanut on a trampoline, calmed a little and replied, 'Yes, yes OK Tilly, that's what we will do.'

CHAPTER NINE

The Task Ahead

Even though the daylight hours hadn't yet reached midday, neither Tilly nor Ash wished to waste any time. Tilly made her way down to the hut and Ash hopped and danced in elation towards his family tree. It was clear Ash found it extremely difficult to contain his bubbling excitement, as he hopped and skipped over the shallow roots which sprawled across the glade like elongated fingers. Back at the hut, Tilly began to think seriously about what she might need for the first attempt at the daunting task ahead.

After placing the scroll down carefully on the workbench, Tilly gathered her notebook and pen. She read the scroll once more and took notes of the most important bits. Talking aloud to herself, she read slowly and methodically as she began to write, 'Stalk of a deadly cap fungus, bark bugs, Arion bird ... Arion bird, what is an Arion bird? Oh, how will I *ever* manage to do all this?' With a subtle sigh of frustration, she paused her writing as doubts crept in and she wondered, just for a moment, if even the first part of the task could be achieved.

Trying to avoid panic, Tilly's questioning nature took over. Even if she didn't succeed, her immense curiosity needed to see what could be done. She understood, in her world, she might be a little bit unconventional, but here she was, chosen to be in this other mystical world which, she thought, must mean something.

For safekeeping, Tilly placed the scroll back into its box, before looking again at her initial notes, pausing at the words bark bugs. She wondered whether they might be the little bugs she had previously watched walking across the glade. She needed to find out. Establishing this had to be her starting point.

The time ticked towards 12 noon and Tilly's stomach had already started giving modest hints it might need some nutrition. Random rumblings sang out like a disorganised amateur choir, so filling up on food seemed her next priority. She consumed her peanut butter sandwich as quickly as she could and drank some of the juice, and while she did so she recalled the first instruction again and again, 'Gather a stalk of the deadly cap fungus. Use the bark bugs and the Arion bird to help you.' Now fed, Tilly headed purposefully back towards the glade.

Ash had gathered food provisions for himself. His small leather foraging bag now encased enough puff seeds to keep his energy levels up during what lay ahead. 'We need to find the bark bugs!' yelled Tilly, as she negotiated the small dislodged pathways to meet with Ash once more, 'they can help us find the deadly cap fungus.'

Ash skipped down from the top of the glade and as the pair met they searched for the bugs. Down on all fours, Tilly scooped the soil and surface twigs around, taking care not to damage any little insects which might be there. But she wasn't sure she was in the right place. She also wasn't entirely sure what the bark bugs looked like. Needing clarity, she checked with Ash, 'Do the bark bugs have curly backs? Are they the bugs that I saw, over there yesterday?' she asked, pointing to an area close by.

Ash smiled. 'Yes of course, they often commute over the glade, but they are so tiny they are hard to see. You were very lucky to spot them.'

With renewed enthusiasm, both realised they had to relocate a little and without hesitation, headed for the spot where Tilly had seen them the day before. The hubbub of living things all around displayed vibrant colours and as Tilly moved towards the new searching area, she couldn't resist the urge to collect some samples along the way. She knew she had packed some pots and a pair of tweezers in her backpack and seeing some pretty thistle-like flowers, a rich blue in colour; she found a pot, retrieved the tweezers and began. Collecting a few delicate petals, along with an accompanying leaf, she remembered the similar flower head Ash had used for dissolving the hut's padlock door. 'Perhaps these are a similar variant,' she thought, but before becoming too side-tracked, she returned the, now full, sample pot and tweezers to her bag and refocused once more on the search for the elusive bugs.

The familiar clusters of dense shrubs with the petite white flowers were so crammed together, there could have been a whole miniscule world beneath them, but Tilly persevered and it wasn't too long before the miniature bugs were discovered. There they were, tramping along in a regimental line, 'Can you speak to the bugs Ash? Ask them about the deadly fungus. That's what we need,' Tilly persisted.

'But I can't, they don't communicate with the Fidgets, or anything else as far as I know.' Ash replied.

'Oh.' Tilly remembered her fascination when she first saw the little creatures, with their curvy bark-like backs. But she felt slightly puzzled, as on her last sighting, there were tiny specks of red on them. Keen to find out, she threw another question towards Ash, 'What was the red blob they seemed to have on them yesterday, Ash?'

Tilly asked about everything, even if it didn't help the cause she still wanted to know everything she could about these wonderful creatures. After a pause, Ash raised his head with a wide smile emerging, like a huge cavity opening across his face.

'That red blob thing you mention is their food source, and it happens to be part of the deadly cap fungus. Of course! They can lead us to what we need!'

Being very careful not to disturb the regimental line, Tilly and Ash crept slowly behind the tiny bugs. A short distance away, at the base of a tree and not too far from the central glade, the bugs changed direction and began to climb, one by one. As they did so, gaining some height, Tilly leaned in closely to see the diminutive remnants of the red spores that had been carried by each bug before. Her fascination continued as she watched the organisation and teamwork of these little creatures, previously unknown to her.

The bugs climbed and became tiny, shrinking, little dots high up in the tree, with Tilly's bending neck straining more as she tried to follow their movements as they disappeared from her sight. Ash took flight and hovered above while the bugs deviated along a narrower branch to the end. Tilly could do no more from the ground, so she stood waiting, full of anticipation. Other trees and their branches had already obscured the view to the bugs' destination, so all Tilly could do was wait.

It seemed far too long before Ash fluttered back down to the ground where Tilly was eagerly waiting. 'Well, where did the bugs go? Did you see the deadly fungus that we need?'

'Yes,' replied Ash, 'but it is right at the end of the tree's top branch and even just the stalk part is too big for me to gather. We need to find a way for you to get up there Tilly. There is also a nest quite near to the fungus, made of twigs and pebbles. I know it is used by an extremely elusive bird, which now is nowhere to be seen.'

Tilly took in what Ash had said and inwardly gulped. How on earth was she to reach the top branch, the one she couldn't even see from the ground? Feeling like they had already come to a dead end, the forlorn pair meandered back to the hut, deep in thought. Neither Ash nor Tilly had any idea what to do next. At least they knew where the deadly cap fungus was, but they had to find a way to gather a piece of the stalk and, it seemed almost impossible to achieve.

Thinking of the next thing to do seemed tricky. Trying to find a solution, Tilly opened her notebook once more. It was almost like her notebook was becoming a sort of comfort blanket for when she needed a bit of a boost. Hoping something written down might help to guide their next move, she turned each page and observed the contents carefully with intense concentration. As she did so, part of the scroll's information popped into her head, 'The scroll says "the mystical hut can serve you well." That has *got* to be a clue! There must be something here we can use to help us reach the fungus.'

Tilly turned another page of the notebook and continued to read, 'wooden pallets, a plastic bottle, old plant pots, smooth pebbles...' and as she continued to read each word, she also remembered, the selection of rope in the wooden box.

With Ash sitting on the edge of the workbench, Tilly opened the lid once more and Grandad's hat was at the top. The unmistakable indigo feather glued to the side, incredibly pristine. Tilly thought about its beautiful sheen and how exceptionally bright it still was, even after being in a wooden box for however long. She removed the hat from the box once again and placed it on the workbench to see the rope. As her needy companion peered in from the side of the box, she grasped the unruly rope bundle to examine it more closely.

Tilly spread the hoard across the floor, for easier examination and one piece proved to be very long, with quite a large hook on the end. She scratched her scruffy fringe as it got in her eyes and she thought, 'I wonder? I wonder if this rope is long enough.'

Ash looked intrigued and asked, 'Long enough for what?'

'To reach the fungus in the tree, let's try it. We might as well have a go.'

Ash didn't need to be asked twice. He had already jumped from the side of the box and grateful for her help, was eager to get going. Tilly plucked the backpack from the floor, to ensure she had her provisions. After all, she didn't really know how long this might take.

A little while later the pair, having retraced their steps, positioned themselves at the base of the tree. With no sign of the bark bugs, they collected their thoughts and began to plan. Both of them bent their necks as far back as they could to try to see the best route to their prize. Tilly thought it amusing and wondered why Ash didn't just fly to assess the best route, but then she appreciated he may have been affirming their comradery, or just doing what they could both do together, seeing as she couldn't fly. As the pair surveyed their options, she held the bundle of rope securely and secretly hoped it would enable their success.

Thinking of the climb ahead, she placed the backpack down at the base of the tree and looked at her weary trainers. Tilly trusted they had enough grip to help her through this impending mission.

She threw the hooked end up as far as she could and when it remained stuck she pulled to check it was secure. Taking in a deep breath, she tied the other end of the rope around her waist and began the daring climb.

On the precarious journey, upon reaching the hooked end of the rope, she needed to throw it further again. While holding on with one arm, Tilly slung the hooked end of the rope, over a branch above her head and slowly pulled herself up once more. It was hard going and after slipping slightly a couple of times, she wasn't sure how confident she was with heights. With perseverance, she gradually climbed, preventing herself from looking down. Near the top, she stopped to catch her breath, as she puffed like a fast steam train moving towards its next station.

Regaining her steady breath, Tilly couldn't fail to look around, albeit briefly, at the incredible diversity. Sounds filled the air like a full delicate orchestra playing in a bustling theatre. As Tilly's arms held tightly around the swaying tree, three pink butterflies floated by with distinct blue markings on their wings, looking like striped candy sweets. They reminded her of the mint humbugs she liked to eat. As she daydreamed, a familiar subtle humming sound came and Ash came into view, hovering to urge Tilly on, 'You are nearly there, come on, let's do this!'

Tilly had to be cautious now; her position so high up in the tree top resulted in a definite swaying in the breeze. She looked along the branch towards the target. In the first instance, her eyes met the unoccupied nest made of twigs and some smooth pebbles which looked similar to those found in the hut. Then, just a little way beyond, Tilly could just about see the top of the deadly cap fungus, with its bright red visibly standing out. Very cautiously, she un-looped the hook from the previous branch and swung it ahead onto a thinner side branch, before beginning to crawl again, very slowly, along the horizontal branch. Regrettably, as she did so, the thinner branch, the same one she now sat astride, began to dip. It soon became an extremely precarious place to be and trying not to look down, Tilly held on with all her might, but every inch she attempted to move forward, the branch shook and dipped a little more.

Not only was the unusual nest and fungus in jeopardy but so was Tilly's welfare. The laws of physics would not allow her to continue. Even though tantalizingly close, the exasperated young adventurer rested, deflated, on the wobbling branch. Holding on tightly, her eyes were drawn to a light source on the ground. It was so far away that she could not fathom what it was but she had no time to consider as the swaying branch brought her rapidly back to perilous moment. It was clear this plan wasn't going to work. Tilly realised she needed to survive and pursue another way, so slowly reversed along the delicate and wobbly branch to reach the main trunk. Steadily, she continued the descent to the ground, where Ash had been waiting, pruning his elegant wings and eating his small stock of puff seeds. By the time Tilly's feet reached the ground, a dozing Ash, lay, curled up beside a silky, feathery fern.

The shining source of light appeared once more and with Tilly's feet firmly on the ground, she tracked the light source to her backpack, placed nearby at the foot of the tree. With a mystified look, she opened the buckle as quickly as she could and rooted for the light source. Picking it up with one hand, she inhaled, holding the intriguing pebble that had been placed in there just the day before.

The sight became hypnotic, staring at the materialising colours, not dissimilar to an opulent rainbow. The mysterious pebble felt warm and extremely smooth. Tilly lifted her hand into the air and as she absorbed the beautiful hues an unfamiliar creature swooped across the woodland floor and landed a few feet away. The creature's abrupt landing shook the ground, making Ash stir from his slumber to see Tilly freeze to the spot.

Ash flew up like a rocket and called out, 'It's Arion! It's Arion!'

CHAPTER TEN

Meeting Arion

Standing just a few feet away loomed a terrifying swan-like creature. Towering above Tilly, the creature's large yellow eyes seemed to penetrate her frozen skin. Tilly's petite frame remained static as her fingers clenched tightly around the pebble, almost as if it were glued. With the creature's eyes still fixed, it tilted its head, just slightly, as if to gain a more intense view.

Still airborne close by, Ash glided, delicately towards the head of the wary creature. As he did so the creature lowered its swan-like neck from the air to meet him. The little imp's presence radiated calm and he and Arion shared a connection as the imposing bird sniffed at him, beginning to relax a little.

'Tilly, this is Arion. He is a very rare but welcome sight. You held one of his sacred pebbles and called him to us.'

Hearing the comforting words, Tilly relaxed a bit and realised she needed to take in a large breath. With her heart still pounding in her panicked, slightly quivering body, she attempted to speak, 'Uh, hello Arion, it's n-nice to meet you.'

The extraordinary bird raised his head and took a step back as he heard Tilly's unfamiliar voice. Ash could see the fearful look in Tilly's face and he quickly tried to reassure her, 'It's OK Tilly; Arion is a very secretive creature and has only ever met one other being from the human world, your grandad. Once he trusts you, he will be a faithful friend to you.'

After a time of quiet contemplation, with the surrounding wildlife carrying on with their daily tasks, Arion and Tilly began to relax in each other's company. She stared up at the incredible creature not quite believing how lucky she felt, to be so near to this elusive bird. Quietly standing, she studied its majestic appearance; with an eagle-like head and jet-black hooked beak, Arion looked imposing and threatening. His large yellow eyes added to his fierce appearance, although with his long neck there was also something quite serene about him. The huge bird stood on strong, stocky legs with large golden talons, and showed long, elegant tail feathers with golden tips. But the most impressive thing, from Tilly's point of view, was his plumage, his deep, shimmering, indigo plumage. It oozed splendour, making him almost noble.

Practically in a daze, Tilly's mind turned into a magical soup, made up of imps and mystical birds and talking flowers. She still couldn't quite believe what had happened in the last couple of days. Just then, Ash interrupted her thoughts, 'Are you OK Tilly? Do you want to come a bit closer to him?'

'Wait, really, can I?' Tilly bubbled up inside with excitement, but was afraid to show her feelings for fear of scaring the bird away.

'Come,' said Ash.

Taking very slow steps forward, Tilly observed the bird's piercing eyes as she moved cautiously, one step at a time towards the huge creature. Then, with the sacred pebble still in her hand, she slowly reached her arm out and presented it to the majestic bird. Arion began to stretch his neck towards the open hand and after a few sniffs, gently removed the pebble with his beak. He then lowered his serene neck to the ground and placed the pebble near to the base of the tree. Just a few seconds later, remarkably, the bird then outstretched his neck once more, close enough for Tilly to be able to touch it. The bond had been made. Arion had invited Tilly to touch him. They could now be friends.

Normally a shy and solitary bird, Arion nested high in the tree tops and along with the tiny bark bugs enjoyed a diet of deadly cap fungus, which wasn't deadly to either the bird or the bugs. As Tilly stroked Arion's plumage, her thoughts became clear. The feathers were precisely the same as the one in Grandad's hat. In the following minutes, Tilly became more relaxed in the bird's company and it was now she understood the special affinity he must have enjoyed with this incredible bird, and now, she hoped, she could experience the same.

Tilly quickly scrunched her eyes up only to open them again, just to check she was still awake and in the moment. Ash landed on her shoulder and whispered, 'Remember the task; we need to gather some of the stalk of the fungus.'

'Yes you are right Ash,' she whispered, 'and this is how we can do it. Arion can help us.'

Thinking about the details in the scroll, Tilly knew the Arion bird somehow played a part in gathering the fungus for the first part of the charm. Patience was needed, but she somehow knew Arion was the key to their success. Arion relaxed more in Tilly's company, until he lowered his neck to the ground and began to gently bump her leg. Tilly asked Ash for guidance, 'Wh-what do I do?'

Ash grinned and replied excitedly, 'Well, it looks like he's ready to take you for a ride. Jump on, jump on!'

A wave of anxiety engulfed Tilly. She had to get this right or it would affect the whole mission. She gingerly accepted Arion's request and she very carefully, lifted one leg over his neck, which seemed as wide as a horse's back. She gradually looped her arms around his neck as Ash said, 'Remember it is the stalk part of the fungus you need and don't touch the red cap, it is deadly!'

As Tilly had looped her arms around the sleek neck, Arion began to take flight. Huge gleaming wings emerged behind Tilly's back and as she looked down at Ash, on the ground, she saw that Arion's talons had dug trench marks in the ground taking off.

Tilly floated above the canopy of the woodland. A carpet of countless greens, dispersed with blobs of unusually bright colours lay beneath her. Arion glided gracefully past his unusual pebbly nest to reach the fungus, where he paused to linger.

The moment had come. Tilly kept one arm wrapped tightly around Arion's neck, while reaching out with the other. Her fingers reached nearly close enough to tickle the fungus plant, but her awareness of the extremely dangerous red cap stayed at the forefront of her mind. Inch by inch, she stretched a little more, leaning almost to the point where she might slip off the bird's back. Finally, her fingertips tickled the spongy stalk of the plant. With a further stretch her fingertips just managed to hoop the stalk towards her. Taking extreme care not to touch the red top, she grasped the stalk and pulled. The action of pulling dislodged the red top, which fell to the side and enabled Tilly to retrieve the stalk in safety.

Wasting no time, she linked her arm back around Arion's magnificent neck and very soon both had landed safely. Carefully dismounting, Tilly calmly stroked Arion's neck once more, 'Thank you so much Arion. We couldn't have done it without you.' Ash also flew up to Arion to salute the achievement. The mystical bird bowed his neck as if to acknowledge the grateful pair, before taking flight once more towards his secluded canopy nest.

Still holding the precious stalk, Tilly reached for her backpack and opened the front pocket for the stalk to go in. She then looked towards the base of the tree where Arion had placed her special pebble. Having already formed quite an attachment to the innate object, Tilly picked it up and placed it in the pocket of her jeans. Then, looking up at the sky, she couldn't be sure if the light was fading or if the clouds had increased, so she needed to check the time once more. She knew she'd eaten her lunch early but with all the excitement, she wanted to be sure she still had time on her side. Amazingly, the time said 1pm. Once again, it was like time had slowed right down while she had been in the woods. Mystified, she looked at Ash, who could see she needed an explanation.

'Well,' he started, 'that would be my cousin species, the Flint fairies. They can slow time down when needed. They are obviously aware of your presence here, even though you may not have seen them yet.'

'How fascinating,' responded Tilly, 'that's brilliant! That means we can continue with the tasks without me worrying all the time about getting home too late. I don't know about you but I could do with a biscuit or two.'

Walking back towards the hut, Tilly felt energised by their accomplishment. 'We've done it, we've actually done it!' she hopped along. 'We've got the first ingredient, woo hoo!'

As the two of them reached the hut, Tilly looked all around and just naturally knew there was more to this magical place, much more. Looking in an unfamiliar direction, she spotted a clearing in the distance. Blinking and wiping her scruffy fringe from her vision once more, she could see the makings of another pathway, with branches acting as signposts along the side of an irregular, gravelly path.

Back in the quirky, damp hut, Tilly scanned for a suitable place to keep the piece of fungus. It needed to be kept safe, until all ingredients had been gathered and so she placed it carefully into the same wooden box as the scroll. Although it had been an eventful few hours, she was even keener to see what the next instruction would be and removing the scroll from the same box, unrolled it once more to take a look. It read, 'Gather a piece of discarded tusk from the Brog's cavern. Use the yarrow white flower to give you sight.'

Ash, still in Tilly's company, listened intently. 'Hhmmm, that sounds extremely challenging for me ... You'll have to find the Brog's cavern first.'

Although part of the magical realm, Ash had never really left the safe protection of the central glade, so he didn't know precisely where the Brog's caverns were. 'Well, I know of dark caverns within ragged cliff faces somewhere, but am not sure in which direction they are,' he said with sadness in his voice, 'and even if I did know, I couldn't go there, I'd be far too scared to come across the Brog himself.'

Seeing the fear in Ash's eyes, Tilly decided the next plan of action might need some thought, so she began to gather the backpack belongings to head home. 'Ash,' she said, 'outside, I just noticed a clearing in the distance with what looks like another pathway. It seems to be going down in the direction of the valley. Could it be an alternative route back to my grandad's place?'

Ash scratched an itch on his bony knee and said, 'It could be. I know your grandad didn't get here using the tunnel under the hut, so there must be another way.'

'Brilliant,' said Tilly, 'I'm going to see where that route takes me. It might be a much quicker way and if it isn't, then I'll just come back here and go through the tunnel under the hut to get home.'

With the notebook and her other things packed up, Tilly stood outside, with the old hut behind her.

She waved to Ash and headed towards the clearing in the distance. It's not long before the branches of the irregular trees seemed to beckon her to keep going as her footsteps echoed crunchy sounds upon a gravelly pathway underfoot. As she walked towards a downhill slope, looking further ahead, Tilly could see the tops of the cottage chimneys popping up just above the next brow as if playing peek-a-boo. Seeing the distant chimneys reassured her of her route, but before that, she found herself at the beginning of a deep ravine. She followed the gravelly path as it headed down a narrow slope and the natural light all around darkened, with the air temperature dropping.

At the bottom of the deep, cold ravine, the terrain became uneven and treacherous. Rocks and boulders were scattered around, like a giant had thrown his clumpy dice across the landscape. Within the eerily cool atmosphere the vibrant wildlife had become subdued into almost silence. Knowing the cottages were just over the next hill, Tilly kept going, through translucent strips of mist that floated randomly in the air, yet she felt an air of dread with every step. At last, the pathway began to climb once more and with a slight bend in the meandering land, a large cliff face came into view. The sky was grey and cloudy as a very edgy Tilly kept her head down focused on each footstep home.

'Ouch!' Something hard hit Tilly's shin and something else struck her knee. Looking down, a small stone had landed on the track beside her and turning to see who threw it, she spotted some movement just behind a nearby boulder. Nervously, she asked, 'Hello, who's there?'

Almost immediately, a small creature poked out from behind the boulder and began to speak, 'I am Saffron, one of the Flint fairies. Your help is needed here. Please wait.'

Still in pain, Tilly crouched to rub her bruised shin more and to see the little soul. After a few seconds of mental adjustment at meeting this new species, Tilly asked, 'Do you live here? Ash told me of the Flint fairies and how you have been helping us with slowing down the time. Goodness knows how you do that, but thanks,' Tilly waited for a response, as Saffron began to show herself little by little, stepping forward into the murky light.

'Yes we can slow down time. It has been a very useful gift in the past and so too again now,' she replied. 'So can you? Can you help here?' Saffron repeated her question.

'I'm not sure. Why do you need *my* help?' Tilly wondered what she could do for this little fairy.

'Look, in the cliff face. There are deep caverns, where my kind live. But we are not alone, and we need your help to save our friend and neighbour, the Brog. He is starving and very soon, will not survive.'

'Wait, what, the Brog ... the Brog lives here? But where is he now? Am I safe?' Tilly began to shuffle away from the cliff face and towards home.

'Do not fear, it's OK, he means you no harm. He is much misunderstood. Look, I know you've had an eventful day so far, but please let me explain. Oh, and you don't need to worry about the time as we have slowed it right down for you. You have at least another hour here and you'll still get home in plenty of time.' Saffron's gentle eyes widened as she waited.

Tilly paused for a moment and considered whether it would be a safe thing for her to do. Honestly, she didn't really know, but felt as Ash's cousin species, it could be supposed that Saffron could be trusted, it was her domain after all. And with a weary nod, Tilly sat down beside a large boulder to listen.

CHAPTER ELEVEN

The Flint Fairies

Saffron, a fairy of slight form, spoke with an easy-going tone and began to tell the plight of the much misunderstood Brog. To other inhabitants of the woodland, his stature portrayed a villain, mighty in nature with a long blunt snout and capable of mass destruction. His appearance could be described as hog-like with sharp white tusks protruding from either side of his hairy nose, with folds of leathery skin draping down his cheeks.

As a nocturnal beast, during most day light hours the solitary Brog would rest within the confines of his cavern, with only an occasional outbound stroll for top-up nibbles of vegetation. Historically, the local community became his worst enemy; with his ancestors hunted down for their precious tusks. In illegal circles, the tusks would be carved into elaborate designs and sold for huge profits, causing giant losses to the scientific field. Each tusk contained a diverse mineral content to include precious calcium, a vital mineral for new life and any opportunity to study the tusks would also provide a valuable record of the animal's lives, as well as essential DNA for genetic studies. The senseless act of human hunting had resulted in the demise of the species, and as far as the Flint fairies were aware, this solitary Brog was the last surviving one. Saffron and the rest of her kind had made it their cause to protect the last beast for the rest of its days.

As Saffron spoke, Tilly drank some juice and observed her closely; the little fairy so very slender, with smooth skin and long, flowing golden hair. Wearing a loose bodice, with multiple fawn-coloured feathers, she blended into the cliff face behind. Saffron seemed generous in nature and practical in approach. 'Look,' she said amicably, 'as far as we know the Brog is all alone and he needs your help. You can help to secure his future existence.' Saffron took a deep breath and continued, 'his staple food is in very short supply. It's a desperate situation, follow me and I'll show you what I mean.' Saffron floated into the air, beckoning Tilly to follow. Pushing herself up from the damp, cold ground, Tilly hesitantly obliged.

Retracing familiar steps around the bend from the cliff face, Saffron led Tilly a little way back towards the old hut, but then, to one side of the gravelly track the land swooped down dramatically onto a lower plain. There were numerous muddy indentations aiming downwards, forming a messy, squelchy pathway, where Saffron was keen to show.

Upon reaching the bottom of the lower plain, Tilly stood looking at what appeared to be a load of old twisted plants that had died off for the winter. 'What are we looking at?' she asked Saffron.

'Unfortunately,' Saffron replied, 'we are looking at the Brog's staple food. These were the main supply of the crimson tassel plants, but in the recent rain storm, the already saturated ground could not cope and with inundated drenching for so long the plants have not survived the boggy ground.' Saffron stood on the top of a wilted tassel head and stared quite seriously at Tilly, who initially didn't know how to respond.

After a few long seconds, Tilly shared her considered reply, 'Why should I help you to help this creature, when he completely destroyed Ash's family home and left Ash distraught and all alone?'

Saffron responded, 'Yes, you are right, but he would not have done that if he were not starving. There is always a plentiful supply of puff seeds and he had no other food source. He was acting in desperation. It was his only way to survive. Honestly, Tilly, that is why more crimson tassel plants are needed and they are needed fast otherwise, it will be too late. The Brog will be extinct.'

Tilly was only too aware of the impact climate change and disrupted weather patterns could have on food chains. She quietly considered the impact to the Brog's existence and then thought about her potential role to help. Here she stood in this strange mystical land and although she wanted to help Saffron and even potentially the Brog, she could not work out how. Saffron spoke again, 'You could ask Ash to help you, knowing how good he is with nurturing plants. I know he won't venture from the safety of the glade, but you can perhaps take the plants to him? Won't you please?' Saffron's easy-going voice was beginning to sound a little desperate.

Tilly tucked some unruly strands of hair behind her left ear and sighed, 'Oh, if only I knew the answers to everything!'

Just then shimmers of sparkly light surrounded her before falling, quite elegantly to the ground and just a few inches away became the familiar sight of Sariel's silvery wings just settling on the mud-covered track. 'Ash can help you that *is* true, but you are the one with the knowledge to do ...' And with that, Sariel left as abruptly as she arrived, leaving the short, unexplained riddle behind her.

Saffron peered at Tilly, full of anticipation. Tilly still had no idea what to do, yet with resignation in the knowledge she needed to do something, tried to reassure the affable fairy. 'OK, so this is something I can *apparently* do, I just don't know what it is yet. I'll head back to see Ash and try to work out how I can help. Do I have enough time to do that?' Tilly enquired, and Saffron, who looked extremely relieved, responded with a simple, Yes please!

Suddenly, Tilly heard more of the familiar whispers behind her. Two more Flint fairies appeared dancing in the air. 'Tilly,' Saffron said, 'here are two of my brothers, Rowan and Dill.'

'We love being able to 'whisper'; it's nice to meet you Tilly,' said Rowan still flitting around in circles with his brother Dill.

Tilly's eyes lit up. 'So you're the whispers, wow! Do all of you whisper?'

'Yes we do,' replied Saffron, 'that's exactly what we did to prevent the hunters from entering the woods over time. That's how we managed to save the final Brog in the end.'

Tilly couldn't contain her amazement and asked the fairies if it were their whispers which helped her to reach the hut, the same whispers that guided her through to the mystical tunnel. She needn't have doubted the response and without wasting any more time, she headed back to see Ash.

As Tilly began the short journey back, Saffron shouted out to her, 'And yes, you have time; we will make sure of that.'

Back at the central glade, Ash appeared to be impatiently attempting to smooth some of the large muddy craters still left since the awful beastly visit. He flitted around in true Fidget fashion and when he looked up, he witnessed an approaching Tilly rubbing her shin. He looked surprised, 'What is it, are you OK?'

'Yes I'm fine, just a little sore,' she replied.

Looking concerned, Ash immediately went to have a look. 'I can sort that out for you, come over here.' Beckoning Tilly to the edge of the stream, the talented imp cupped some flowing water into his wide, bony hands to sprinkle onto the bruise. He then just touched, very gently and the pain began to disperse.

'That feels much better. Thank you, Ash,' Tilly said with a warm smile.

Ash looked pleased and then asked, 'Didn't that route go anywhere? I guess you couldn't find your cottage that way then.'

'No, you are sort of right, I couldn't. But I did meet the Flint fairies and you and I must help the Brog,' Tilly responded.

'Help the Brog! What! After he decimated my home and split me up from the rest of my family? What do you mean we have to help the Brog?' Ash was steaming mad. His normally pale cheeks were now bright red and his spindly arms were thumping the air fiercely like a master drummer banging on invisible drums.

Tilly hurriedly stepped back, unsure of what to say or do next. 'I can explain, Ash, let me explain. Meet me at the hut when you feel like it, please it's important.'

Not having seen Ash so angry before, Tilly felt sad that she had even mentioned helping the Brog, yet she knew, morally, it had to be the right thing to do. Quickly, she retreated to the hut, where she sat on her log seat to wait for a calmer Ash. While she waited, she thought about the problem; the Brog needed lots of crimson tassel plants to survive and somehow, Tilly and Ash needed to achieve that.

For a while now, Tilly had completely forgotten about the quest within the scroll. Staring up onto the workbench, it jolted her memory of why she was there. In lots of ways she could understand Ash's fury with any suggestion to help the Brog. But with what Saffron had said, Tilly felt different. The Brog acted in desperation after all. Tilly thought about her passion for all living things and then she thought about helping the misunderstood beast. It would be incredible, to be responsible for preventing an animal from becoming extinct. *'How amazing that would be.'*

Still waiting for Ash, Tilly opened the wooden box to have another look at the scroll. Before she touched it, she looked again at the two loose photographs in the box. Each picture showed pots of green saplings, just a couple of inches high. Each plant had an unusual shape with twisted stems, reminding her of a corkscrew bottle opener which she had seen her parents use at dinner parties. On both images Tilly could just about make out emerging orangey-red flowers at the end of each stem, which hung down in a cluster. These saplings looked familiar to her and it didn't take long before she realised they were the same as the ones Saffron had just presented, the crimson tassel plants. Looking again, each photograph also showed a few smooth pebbles lying randomly beside the plants. Tilly studied the background and recognised the setting within the hut itself. Looking across to the back wall of the hut, the selection of pots was still there with evidence of dried-up saplings within. Reaching down to gather a pot, she looked more closely and the twisted stems showed interesting art forms, in the shape of twig sculptures. Each sapling looked well beyond its best, yet it was clear they were the same plant.

Still studying the little plant now sitting on the workbench under the window, Tilly wondered how long the dusty pots had been there. At least she now knew what was so special about them. She decided to keep the two photographs and carefully placed them in her pocket alongside the others.

At that moment, a subtle noise came from the split in the wooden door and as she looked around, she saw Ash squeezing through to meet her, 'I'm still fuming mad, but I'll listen to what you want to say,'

Ash spouted as he jumped onto his spot under the window.

Relieved Tilly wasted no time in explaining, 'So ... Saffron said that the Brog is near to extinction. As far as she can tell, there is only the one Brog left. You must know the only reason he attacked your glade was in desperation for food, he had no choice. Saffron specifically said you and I could help him; we could prevent this misunderstood creature from his demise. But I can't do it on my own Ash, what do you think?'

A long silence ensued. Ash remained quite still on the workbench and fiddled with his foraging bag, his bony leg swinging back and forth off the side of the ledge. The seconds ticked by ... Tilly became impatient and spoke again with frustration in her voice, 'Well, if you're not going to help, I'll just have to do it on my own!'

Ash hopped up, 'No wait! I now understand the beast needs our support and if it helps me get another step closer to my family, then that's what we will do. What do we need to fix?'

Again, Tilly felt huge relief. She knew she couldn't do anything without Ash, but didn't want to admit that. She paced up and down the small space within the hut with renewed enthusiasm and announced, 'I think I've worked out what we need to do. We need to bring those plants to life and grow them quickly. The Brog's main food source in the ravine, the crimson tassel plants, have died and I have a feeling that those saplings in the pots over there are what he needs.' Tilly pointed to the shrivelled-up plants. 'If only there was a quick way to bring the plants back to life,' she said.

Tilly searched the cardboard boxes for a waterproof container. She needed to collect some water from the nearby stream to water the saplings. It was a long shot, but she hoped there might be tiny green shoots which may be encouraged to sprout when watered. She failed to even notice Ash, who sat patiently waiting for her to take a breath and make eye contact.

Ash said, with a much more enthusiastic tone, 'I can revive and nurture the plants, once they've had some of the restorative stream water Tilly. I have a feeling the scroll mentions the Brog, we should check to see.'

'That's amazing; you seemed to know what my thoughts were then,' Tilly said encouragingly. 'I think we can do this Ash!' And with those words, she grabbed an old plastic container and headed for the glade.

CHAPTER TWELVE

The Greater Good

It felt virtuous to be sprinkling the refreshing water around each withered stem and as Tilly did so she wished the plants could talk and tell of the tales spent with her grandad in the past. A little saddened, but with a renewed hope, she urged the little plants to come to life. She also gave them an informative 'talk' to explain why they were so needed and while she did so, she considered the Flint fairies feelings for their close friend, the Brog.

Tilly completely understood the Flint fairy's mission to look after the Brog and how it brought them a meaningful existence, a purpose for the greater good. Life was complex, for everyone and everything, but recognising every being as a small cog in the vast mechanics of the beautiful planet, only served to enrich life. Having spent time within the Fidgets magical realm, Tilly could see Ash's natural affinity for the wondrous plant kingdom. She could also see the Flint fairy's closeness with the animals. It worked; different species helped each other, with the Brog accommodating the Flint fairies in his space, to protect them from the dangerous elements outside.

As Tilly watered the final sapling, she assumed Grandad's role may have been like hers right now, perhaps also helping the Brog, before the awful day arrived, when Grandad would no longer return to the mystical Whispering Wood.

Tilly placed the empty watering container onto the floor and stood back. Ash hopped down from the workbench to join her. The row of shrivelled saplings lapped up the juice, seemingly slurping every drip into their roots, but because they were so dry, little trails of surplus water leaked out from the base holes and formed a network of twisting streams across the floor. The first part of the nurturing plan had been completed. Now all Tilly could do was hope that Ash could work his magic in time.

With the watering done, the pair pursued the scroll once more. They needed to clarify the second ingredient of the charm, so Tilly unravelled the delicate edges once more and read, 'Gather a piece of discarded tusk from the Brog's cavern. Use the yarrow white flower to give you sight.'

Just as before, with mention of the Brog, Ash went very pale and gulped, 'S-sorry Tilly, but I can't even think about entering the Brog's cavern, that's just madness! I'd be eaten!'

'It does sound rather scary,' Tilly said. 'But the Flint fairies live there and they are OK.'

Ash stayed silent and shook his head, 'Nope, no way, absolutely not!'

'OK, I hear you,' Tilly said, 'but if we can get the crimson tassel plants to grow, then maybe the Brog will let us. Anyway, I'm afraid I need to get going. I really must get home. Perhaps you can help to revive the plants; it seems that's what we need to do, before we can do anything else.' And with that, she began her purposeful journey home.

Choosing to take the quickest route, she passed the chilly cavern once more and reached the brow of the hill. All was quiet and this time, this journey, she saw no sign of the Flint fairies or the mighty Brog. A short distance from the other side of the meandering landscape, the back of the cottages came into view. After the day Tilly had experienced, she smiled at the very welcome sight.

A short while later, and with the woodland behind her, Tilly pushed through the stiff garden gate. She could not wait to rest on her creaky bed and take in the events of the day. Walking up the uneven pathway, she checked her watch to see it approaching nearly 2pm. With a little anxiety, and creeping towards the cottage back door, she wondered, just for a moment, if her family had already returned. She tentatively peered through the small window into the kitchen and there appeared to be no movement. Carefully taking the key from its hiding place to unlock the door, Tilly imagined herself a detective, creeping around trying to solve a crime.

Once inside, she listened but heard no sound. Just to be sure, she ran on tip toes through the front room to the front window beside the main cottage door. She looked onto the road at the space where the family car usually was but the space was empty.

It looked like Tilly had made it back, just as Saffron had said, before everyone else. Saffron was right, the

Flint fairies really *had* slowed the time right down. Walking back to the rear step, Tilly removed her dirty trainers from her feet and after pouring a large glass of lemonade, she went to her room.

It was time to scrutinise the day's events and recall the achievements. With a lot to think about, Tilly opened her backpack and delved inside for the notebook, 'First things first,' she said to herself with authority. She needed to keep things updated. Thinking about the events of the day, she felt she had been in a fast-paced animation film, full of exhilaration and excitement.

Tilly opened the notebook at the last entry and realised it had been written only a few hours before, in the morning of her arrival in Whispering Wood yet, to Tilly, it felt like almost a week ago. She scanned the writing, 'stalk of the deadly cap fungus, bark bugs, Arion bird.' She couldn't quite believe what she had achieved, with the help of her intrepid imp friend.

She wrote down the memorised second instruction from the scroll, 'Gather a piece of discarded tusk from the Brog's cavern. Use the yarrow's white flower to give you sight.' She recorded her notes highlighting the main events of the day. She put her notebook down and feeling quite exhausted, lent back on her cosy bed and began to doze.

The front door banged and shrill voices filled the sleepy cottage, awakening Tilly. The family had returned from their cinema and lunch trip and the golden silence was shattered.

The sound of footsteps approached closer and closer, navigating the stairs to just outside Tilly's room. The wobbly door handle moved slightly as the door slowly opened. 'Hi love, have you been OK today? Did you manage to do any sorting out in the attic?' Mum asked as she stood in the doorway.

'Yes, I've been fine thanks, but no, I didn't get time to do any attic stuff,' she replied.

'Oh, OK, well at least you've had some peace and quiet while we've all been out.' And as she spoke, Mum slowly closed the bedroom door once more.

'Hhmmm, little does she know what peace and quiet I've had,' Tilly thought. For the rest of the afternoon, she carefully considered the next stage of the scroll mission in partnership with Ash. She also thought about the moment the scroll had been found and remembered finding her grandad's binoculars. She reached for her backpack resting alongside her bed. Pulling them out, she could still not believe what a lucky find she had made. She held so many fun memories of her imaginary exploring using her imaginary binoculars alongside her grandad using this special pair. Holding them in her hands, Tilly wrestled with her conscience as to whether she should or should not actually use them for herself, now he was no longer here. After a while, she decided her grandad would want her to use them. After all, as a budding nature scientist, he would encourage her to use all that was available to her for the benefits of scientific research.

So, Tilly raised the binoculars to her eyes, hoping to scan in closely at the spider's web in the corner of the ceiling. At first the view seemed a little blurry, but as Tilly adjusted the central dioptre, the image became clear. Expecting to see the artistic web in more detail, she slumped back upon her bed, so quickly she almost banged her head on the wall behind. Instead of showing the spider's web, Tilly could see Ash moving carefully around the dried-up saplings within the rustic hut. Not quite understanding the vision before her, she brought the binoculars to her knees just for a moment, before raising them to her eyes once more. Again, there was Ash moving around, nurturing the saplings, in the same place Tilly had left him just a short while before.

'What was going on here?' Tilly thought. Still staring through the lenses, she realised that the binoculars provided a view into the Fidget world in the here and now. 'Wow!' she whispered aloud. 'It's no wonder my grandad never let me use these, they are magical!'

Wanting to get a clearer view, Tilly adjusted the central dioptre a little more and as she did so something even more incredible happened. The image of Ash dispersed and a new image appeared. After a few seconds, Tilly gasped as she began to realise what she could now see. A cluster of Fidgets, just like Ash, were sitting in a circle holding hands. She held her breath as she continued to stare, without blinking, but within seconds the image reverted to show Ash once more. Not knowing what to think, Tilly rested on her bed. Was her mind playing tricks on her, or did she just see some of Ash's family, wherever they now were? She struggled to decide whether she should tell Ash or not. 'What if the scroll mission fails and he never gets to see his family again, surely he would want to know they were OK? Or maybe if I did tell him, it would jeopardise the whole quest in some way and somehow prevent it succeeding?' Tilly was unsure and quickly placed the binoculars away. Her thoughts moved towards the next day's plan. She planned to meet Saffron first thing the next morning. She needed to do that on her way back to the hut to inform her of the saplings which Tilly and Ash hoped to revive.

Later, nearing teatime, Tilly helped in the kitchen. Mum liked to make spaghetti Bolognese, which was always a family favourite. Tilly cleaned and chopped the peppers and onions ready for the frying. Although she liked to help with the cooking, she disliked eating sweet pepper which she took out of her meals and lined up around the edge of her plate, to the annoyance of her mother.

The evening dragged. Tilly watched some television, but kept drifting off in a dream about what was to come the following day. She wondered how long it would take for the saplings to grow and how easy it would be to replant them. She prayed for a positive outcome which would result in the Brog allowing access to his cavern, but Tilly knew she and Ash would have to gather some of the yarrow white flowers first. Feeling slightly overwhelmed, her thoughts were interrupted when Mum said, 'Tilly, as you know, there is a lot to do while we are here. Tomorrow, your sisters are heading back home, by bus to prepare themselves for Pony Club Camp. Your dad and I are going to start sorting out Grandad's garage. Tilly? Did you hear me?'

Tilly responded, 'Yes, of course, yes that's OK. I'm quite happy entertaining myself here. You don't need to worry about me.'

The timing couldn't be more perfect. Tilly's older sisters would be going home and Mum and Dad would be away from the cottage and garden, rummaging through Grandad's garage, which was in a row of garages, at the other end of the road. The coast was clear for another day of bold adventures!

CHAPTER THIRTEEN

Crimson Tassels

Tilly awoke full of enthusiasm for the day ahead. She dressed in record time and rested her backpack on top of the bed, ready to fill. With condensation dripping down the inside of the windows, it appeared to be quite a chilly morning; down in the kitchen Mum stood against the warm Aga, having just made a large saucepan of porridge, which now rested, waiting to be consumed.

With relish, Tilly devoured a large portion. Knowing it would more than likely be an eventful day, she needed energy for what might lay ahead. As she ate the final mouthfuls, her older sisters said goodbye and left, laughing like a pair of hyenas, heading for the bus stop at the end of the road. Dad, busy on the phone, confirmed the timing of the delivery of a local skip, to Grandad's garage later that day. It was clearly going to be a busy day for everyone, but Tilly felt sure that hers would be the most exciting.

'We'll be heading off soon Tilly, are you sure you don't want to help us?' Mum asked as she wiped down the draining board.

Tilly looked up and replied, 'I'm happy to stay here, I have lots to keep me busy.'

'If you are sure then you know where we are if you need us. I know you can look after yourself.' And with that, Mum smiled before heading upstairs.

Things were getting a little frantic as Dad was already putting on his work boots. To be fully prepared, Mum had made a flask and sandwiches which lay waiting on the kitchen side. Another sign telling Tilly her parents didn't plan on returning to the cottage, unless they really had to. She just had to wait until the moment she was alone.

Sitting quietly upon her bed, Tilly's parents closed the front door behind them, so she scooped up the backpack and accompanying notebook and headed for the kitchen. As she searched for provisions, she decided to make a cheese spread sandwich, using her usual choice of two slices of white bread. She thought about her favourite accompaniment, ring-shaped snack as she packed the sandwich into her backpack. Tilly very much enjoyed fitting her fingers into the oval crisps to transport every single hoop on their final journey to her mouth. Delving into the back of the larder, she managed to find a packet of her hooped crisps, an apple and a banana too. With the large water bottle full of orange juice, Tilly was ready to go.

Without looking back, she went to the caverns. The cold, autumnal air caused Tilly's face to turn pink as she continued on her way. It didn't take long before the cliff face came into view. She cautiously approached the spot where Saffron had previously appeared. Even though Tilly knew the Brog should now be sleeping, she still felt edgy in the area. She stopped as she reached the large boulder where she had met Saffron the day before. Looking around, everything was calm with familiar birdsong in the air and a gentle breeze tickling the delicate leaves on the branches. Tilly observed the occasional trickle of bronze-coloured leaves falling. After a cold night, patches of frost still rested on the damp earth and the cliff face was moist and cold to the touch.

Tilly didn't know whether to just wait there or try to call Saffron. She considered the Flint fairies might know she was there anyway and that Saffron would soon appear. Sure enough, after a short pause Saffron popped up from behind the boulder, with a welcoming smile.

'Thank you for meeting me again, what news do you have?'

Tilly smiled at Saffron's welcome. 'Well,' she said, 'Ash and I have already started to nurture some saplings in the hut. I left them with Ash once I had watered them.'

Saffron jumped up onto the top of the boulder in sheer delight, 'That's brilliant news!' The little fairy skipped on the spot as she continued, 'As you know it's vital we get these crimson tassel plants to a sustainable size, as quickly as we can. The Brog is getting weaker and weaker and needs a substantial meal to survive. I wasn't sure it could be done, but now I can begin to hope that it might actually be possible.'

Feeling a sense of achievement that her efforts were going to help, Tilly began to head off to see Ash when Saffron shouted after her, 'Wait! Before you go there are more desperate saplings here. If you collect them now, you can take them back with you.'

Tilly wondered if Saffron meant the rotten plants on the lower plain, the decayed ones in the sodden ground. But no, it wasn't those at all. Frantically beckoning Tilly to take a look, Saffron skipped towards the cliff face and then flew up to some interesting crevices halfway up, just above a layer of rock, jutting out like a deliberate shelf. 'Look, these are trying to grow here, birds must have transported the seeds from the lower plains, but they cannot grow to their full size, and anyway they are inaccessible to the Brog. Please take them to Ash where they can be nurtured to full health. Please, Tilly please.'

In the next moment, whispers could be heard in the distance. 'They are calling me,' said the anxious fairy. And with that, she was gone.

Once again, Tilly found herself in a predicament. Should she go straight to Ash, who would probably be waiting for her by now, or should she attempt to retrieve the stunted plants from the crevices first? Tilly stared up at the protruding rock shelf jutting out from the cliff face and attempted to estimate how high it could be from the ground. She was never very good at maths at school, but looking up she thought it would probably be about three times her height. On the last measurement, Tilly recalled her height as around 4ft 10in. Rounding it up to the nearest whole number, she reckoned the shelf may have been as much as 15ft above the ground.

Preferring to think about it as three times her height, it didn't seem as bad and after a few moments of contemplation, Tilly's practical nature won through; she figured she would save time if she collected the plants straight away, rather than seeing Ash and returning. With her decision made, she surveyed the rock face, to imagine the steps where her feet might climb. The more she looked, the more she felt that it should be OK. With lots of jagged rocks as potential handholds and Tilly's deep waistcoat pockets, able to accommodate the freed needy plants, once removed from their cramped crevice home, all was set for the climb.

Standing at the bottom of the cliff, Tilly prepared herself. Being aware of the damp, potentially slippery rock face, she checked the bottom of her trainer's tread for adequate grip. Each foot needed a bit of a kick against the rocks to free bits of mud previously trapped in the grooves. Tilly wondered how each plant might be uprooted, once she had reached the awkward destination and she hoped they would be easy to pull up by hand. Eager to get moving, she took the first step on the craggy face. Keeping her concentration, things appeared to start off quite well. The agile and determined tomboy liked a physical challenge and this was certainly that.

Making the ascent, Tilly felt a bit like a crab negotiating a coastal cliff, and soon enough her hands had reached the rocky ledge. Moving her feet up a little further, the saplings came into view. She thought how strange they looked huddled together, as if preventing one another from falling over the ledge. Along the ledge, Tilly noticed some quite large crevices which easily accommodated seeds from bird transportation or even the wind.

Tilly clung onto the cliff face, quite a distance from the ground, staring at roughly nine or ten saplings bunched together in their ragged, harsh environment. Holding onto the ledge with one hand, she pulled at a sapling with the other, but it didn't budge. She hadn't considered the strength of the roots, or indeed how far they might have buried themselves into the rock face. She pulled again, but the only thing that came away was a couple of the leaves. 'Blast!' she said.

Still holding on, the frustration built. She needed to gather these plants and had to remain calm to work out how it could be done. With the autumnal breeze swirling around, she was cold. The breeze swished through her untidy hair brushing strands across her face, so with her free hand, she wiped it to the side. As she pushed the irritating hair she felt her bootlace necklace. 'Yes, perfect!' Tilly had found her solution. The piece of flintstone seemed ideal to use as a mini-trowel to dig out the roots. Still holding onto the ledge with one hand, she held her flintstone and pulled with the other. It didn't free it, so fumbling around with her free hand Tilly gradually unravelled the knot at the nape of her neck taking great care the lace did not fall.

With the mini 'trowel' in her hand, Tilly's legs were beginning to ache and she knew she needed to be quick, as she didn't know how long she could cling on for. With the flint now in her free hand, she got to work. She dug down under the first sapling trying to keep some of the roots intact. After some resistance and some gentle pulling she successfully freed the hardy plant. Breathing a sigh of relief, she celebrated her first victory with a whispered, 'Yes, Success!' Tilly placed the plant into her inside pocket and continued with the second and then the third.

At full stretch, Tilly needed to adjust her position. It allowed a good opportunity to gain some movement and circulation in her legs and hands. As she shuffled along sideways she imagined herself once more as a hermit crab, this time crawling along a sandy beach around a busy rock pool. With perseverance and patience nine plants were collected and crammed into Tilly's two deep pockets inside her very useful waistcoat. There was just one more to get, but it appeared tricky. Maybe the fact that Tilly could no longer feel her legs didn't help. 'I'm almost there, just one more ...'

Giving herself some encouraging words, Tilly stretched her arm and sliced at the roots. She pulled once more, but as she did so she could not hold on any longer, her cold, stiff fingers let go and she fell through the air, landing on the ground below with a hard thud.

'Ooohh, what just happened?' Tilly found herself at the foot of the climb with the final plant tantalizingly just beside her. Feeling extremely sore she lay partly face down and reached for her painful knee. 'Ouch!' Feeling a little dizzy, she rested her head on the damp ground.

The next few minutes became more and more misty to Tilly. With her eyes closed, she seemed to want to sleep but knew she mustn't. She needed to get back to Ash, and soon. The pain in her knee throbbed, like a lighthouse flashing constantly, with more intensity at each flash. Tilly began to shake, not from the shock, but from the cold. The surrounding temperature had dropped dramatically. She tried to lift herself but pain prevented her. To make matters worse, something else was not right. The natural sounds around had hushed and the atmosphere changed. *What was going on?*

CHAPTER FOURTEEN

The Brog

At this time, following his nightly forage, the Brog would normally be sound asleep. As Tilly lay dazed and in pain, with the clock ticking towards mid-morning, in these uncertain times for his own survival, the Brog had been breaking his sleep pattern for vital nourishment. And he was stirring from deep within the cavern.

Snuffling and snorting, he emerged from his safe space not too far from Tilly, who lay injured, defenceless and scared. The Brog, equipped with razor-sharp tusks around his prickly snout, began to purposefully sniff the space. With an air of intelligence, the creature could not be underestimated. Moreover, his behaviour could also be dangerously unpredictable and, smelling something different within his territory, he persisted along his pathway, clumsily, yet stubbornly, towards Tilly.

Still aware of her surroundings, Tilly lay very still. She fully recognised how hungry the Brog would be and knew this would cause him to turn on anyone or anything close by. She listened intensely to the snuffling behind her. She thought about Ash and the scroll mission and could sense the whole quest slipping into jeopardy. Realising the imminent danger, she didn't know how to get out of it.

Tilly could do nothing more but close her eyes and hope. She grasped at her special pebble tucked neatly into the corner of her jeans pocket, hoping for comfort and with scrunched up eyes, she waited for the looming attack. The Brog stepped ever closer, with the ground trembling under every step, but then, with a weird floating feeling, Tilly had a tickling sensation beneath her. It increased in intensity and as she looked she saw purple feathers emerging and multiplying from underneath her. In no time at all, a whole bed of indigo feathers launched Tilly into the air. She floated along serenely and as she looked down, the Brog ferociously uprooted her previous resting area.

Dazed and perplexed, Tilly closed her eyes once more. By the time she opened them she had been returned to the central glade and found herself lying alongside the energising stream. Ash, now close by, rested his gentle healing hands on her knee and blocking out the natural light above was Arion. A short while later, as Tilly slowly opened her eyes Arion bowed his eagle-like head to within her reach. She managed to stroke his neck for a short while before he stepped back and launched for the sky once more, leaving a purple feather at her feet.

'What ... what just happened?'

'It's alright, you are safe now,' replied Ash. 'Thankfully, you summoned the Arion bird in your hour of need.'

'Did I? What did I do? I remember falling from the cliff face, but how did I get here?'

'Why, the pebble of course, your special pebble. It's one of Arion's from his nest. When you held it, Arion felt the connection and knew you were in danger. Now all we have to do is heal your knee, then we can continue,' Ash smiled.

Tilly was too tired to ask any more questions and knowing she was safely within the protected glade, she rested her head, feeling a lot calmer, as Ash tended to her knee. It felt strange but the central glade always seemed a lot warmer than the rest of the woodland and Tilly soon drifted to sleep.

When she awoke, she felt like she had been asleep for ages, but in fact, it had only been twenty minutes. Recalling what had happened, she glanced at her knee, expecting to see her talented friend, but he was no longer there. Tilly sat up cautiously, thinking of her damaged knee, yet the pain had gone and within a few seconds, she realised she was back to full health. With a deep sigh of relief, Tilly felt an overwhelming sense of gratefulness for her friend's warmth and care.

Tilly stood up and she saw the purple feather resting on the ground beside her. Retrieving the feather, she stroked its soft fringe plume and admired its deep indigo sheen. She placed it tenderly into her top pocket and then scanned the glade for movement. Looking across towards the top of the glade, it didn't take long to spot Ash scurrying around tidying up plants near the ancient family tree, just close to where the raised roots met the grass. Ash certainly could be described as a perfectionist. Tilly watched him settle every leaf of every plant he touched as he continued to nurture his domain back to full health.

'Ash, Ash, I'm OK now, thanks, you are just great!' Tilly called out happily as she ran towards him.

Looking up, he dipped his head, as if to acknowledge Tilly's kind words, 'You must come and see the saplings in the hut,' he replied.

As they walked back towards the hut, they passed the familiar white flowers and Tilly remembered they had a role in words on the scroll. She didn't say anything, but thought she would check the scroll, just to prevent any mistakes.

Back at the hut, the saplings Tilly had left the day before, in Ash's care, were looking good. He had been tending to them for most of the night and they were nearly fully grown. 'That's just astounding! How do you do that Ash?' she asked.

The small clusters of four healthy plants were ready to take to the Brog. And, not only that, but in the pipeline for regeneration were the little saplings in Tilly's deep pockets. Each sapling had to be carefully removed, one by one from her very muddy pockets. It didn't matter to Tilly that her pockets were so muddy; it was her explorer waistcoat after all.

Reaching for the last, she counted and there were nine. Thinking about why the tenth sapling was left behind, Tilly felt slightly disappointed. 'But wait! Perhaps that could have been a good thing,' she thought, as the Brog was so desperately hungry, the sapling on the ground could have been consumed, which in the short term would, she hoped, have saved him.

With her mind still focused upon saving the nine newly collected saplings, Tilly dived into the cardboard boxes and, with help from Ash, scooped out suitable pots to plant them up. It was useful to have found the old bag of gardening compost. It wasn't long before all nine scraggly saplings were ready for watering and to be cared for by the master himself, as Tilly thought.

Tilly's stomach rumbled. With the constant tension from the morning, she needed to replenish her energy. She understood a little of what it felt like for the Brog sensing real hunger, although she knew she wasn't starving by any means.

Being just past eleven in the morning Tilly delved into her backpack to fill up on food. She thought it was sensible to prepare for the journey back to the unexplored internal caverns. First, she placed her cheese spread sandwich and ringed crunchy crisps onto the not-so-clean workbench. Then she retrieved her drinks bottle.

After this short pause to refuel, Tilly checked the details within the scroll, once again. Every time she opened the wooden box, her heart jumped with excitement as she contemplated her role in this new, magical world. She wanted to see what was written about the white flowers. Getting everything exactly right was imperative to the success of the whole charm-making task.

Tilly looked carefully at each word, 'Gather a piece of discarded tusk from the Brog's cavern. Use the yarrow white flowers to give you sight. So that's it!' she said aloud. Tilly knew the white flowers had a vital part to play. Without them, she would not be able to see inside the cavern to collect the second ingredient for the charm.

The plan seemed relatively clear and Tilly already knew the next step involved befriending the Brog with the renewed crimson tassel plants. If that could be accomplished then she assumed she would be allowed entry to the deep cavern where he slept. The Brog simply had to trust what she needed to do; otherwise, the whole quest might fail. With the plan in place, the pair considered their next move as they stared questioningly at one another.

'Ash, we need to get some yarrow flowers, you know, the white flowers on the glade? They will give me sight. Firstly though, I need to put the scroll back safely,' Tilly said as she glanced at the stalk of the deadly cap fungus, just before closing the lid.

Back at the cottage, areas of Grandad's back garden were inundated with yarrow plants and so Tilly knew quite a lot about the small, interesting herb. Growing merrily in the lawn, it held many secrets. The aerial parts were edible and contained many vitamins. The robust plant also held anti-inflammatory properties which mankind had appreciated for centuries, along with other healing benefits. Some people believed it could help ward off evil spirits when mixed with other herbs. After writing many notes and researching botany books in the local library back home, Tilly knew a lot about this green and white treasure within the landscape. Ash could also claim quite an extensive knowledge of the plant too. Although modest, Tilly could sense he was proud of his understanding and connection with the plant kingdom.

Having chosen a suitable container from those in the hut, Tilly and Ash moved swiftly towards the necessary plants. As a large entangled group, the plants appeared to huddle together like a group of penguins facing the elements. Such an interesting plant to observe with tiny bunches of white flowers on tall stems above an abundance of frilly green leaves. Each plant attracted a zoo of insects and Tilly imagined them having the allure of a honey pot, to draw insects in their hoards. With enthusiasm, she picked several of the white flowers, a whole cluster at a time, as she wondered exactly *how* they would give her sight.

'Ash, what do we have to do with these to give me sight? The scroll doesn't explain, it's a mystery to me.' Tilly said. Then, just as Ash's perplexed look showed her that he didn't know either, out of nowhere, curtains of glittering light showered down all around. Wafts of air continued to swoop by until the sparkly lights dispersed on the ground. While fluttering her silver, shimmery wings, the recently absent, gentle-spoken butterfly said, 'You are both doing so well. You certainly are a good team. You are on the right track. Keep going.' And once again, Sariel disappeared in a flick of cool air.

'Oh, she's done it again! Why doesn't she tell us what we need to know?' Ash cried out in frustration. 'I know a lot about yarrow, but what I don't know is what to do with it to give you sight in the dark Tilly!' Ash pounded up and down on the windy pathway liked an irritated grasshopper with an unwelcome flea.

Trying to calm the situation, Tilly responded, 'Look Ash, Sariel said we are on the right track.

Let's look more closely at the scroll's instructions, we must be missing something. It'll be OK, Ash.' Tilly tried to reassure the frustrated imp, even though she hadn't entirely convinced herself. 'Why don't you get some more water for the new saplings and I'll go back to the hut with these flowers and see what I can work out?' Tilly pointed Ash in the direction of the stream and he reluctantly submitted, beating the ground with his bony feet as he went.

With the scroll in her grasp once more, Tilly stared at the contents. She read the words very carefully. Reaching the third verse from the top, she stopped. She reread the verse a second time and then a third:

Have faith that this can be done,
For you have been chosen as the one,
Use your knowledge and your friends,
And keep the hope for a good end.

The words 'use your knowledge and your friends' kept swirling around in Tilly's head. 'Someone or something I have met must surely be able to help. OK, so it's not Sariel, it can't be Arion as I haven't heard him speak; Old Hooky the mole is nowhere to be seen, what else or who else is there?'

Tilly thought hard. Then it hit her. On the first day she entered the central glade she remembered one of the delicate feathery ferns lining the side of the pathway and how it had unfolded in front of her to speak. It had said, 'Tilly, you are one of us now.' *Surely, the same fern could help now*. Thinking it was worth a try, she made the short walk up the glade's pathway to the spot next to the ferns, catching her breath as she paused. Checking where she recalled the blue flower head, without hesitation, she spoke out loud, 'Hello, blue flower head, can you help me? It's Tilly.'

No sooner than the words were spoken one of the fern's leaves began to uncurl and as Tilly stood back in astonishment, the small blue flower emerged. Tilly nervously waited for the flower to speak. 'Ah Tilly, it's so nice of you to see me, I was expecting you. You've already faced some challenges and you have not disappointed us in the way you have overcome them. What can I help you with?'

'Well,' Tilly said taking a deep breath, 'I need to know what to do with the white flower, so I can see inside the Brog's cavern. Please tell me. I don't know who else to ask.'

'That's easy to answer for you. You just eat them, slightly crushed to aid digestion of course. The effects last a couple of hours, which should give you plenty of time to achieve your task and remember you are one of us now.' The small blue flower tucked itself away as quickly as it had come out. Not wanting to forget what the flower had said; Tilly headed straight back to the hut.

In no time at all, the yarrow flowers were ready to consume. Tilly had used the handle of an old gardening trowel to ensure all the flowers were slightly crushed, ensuring she followed the flower's instructions to a 'T'.

All was set for the next part of the plan, but Ash could not be seen. 'Surely he has collected the water from the stream by now?' Tilly thought. Not wishing to lose momentum, she wanted to get going with the four fully grown plants for the Brog. She felt sure he would appreciate his good meal and trust her to have access to his cavern. Gaining his trust was vital to the next part of the plan. Tilly needed Ash, so where was he?

Turning towards the hut door to go and look, she glanced down and there, propped up beside one of the dusty wellies, was a tiny bundle of imp, with his water container by his side. He looked so exhausted and Tilly felt an immense burst of sympathy. Here he sat, all alone, without any of his family, isolated and scared, dreadfully hoping that everything would come right in the end. It must have been difficult to keep going; to keep positive about the future, with so much uncertainty. With a small tear running down her cheek, Tilly knew she had to invest all her strength and determination to help the amazing creature she was privileged to be with.

CHAPTER FIFTEEN

Cavern Adventure

While Ash slept, Tilly took the opportunity to refuel. She ate her banana first, then her juicy apple and finished off with a quick drink. The nibbled apple core, she put beside the cardboard boxes at the back of the hut for the resident mice to find. As she moved within the hut, she must have disturbed Ash, for as she returned to her log he awoke.

He stretched his wafer-thin arms above his head before rubbing his eyes to focus. 'I didn't realise I had gone to sleep,' he said. 'What's been happening?'

'Well, Tilly began, 'I found out what to do with the yarrow flowers and they are now prepared. I must eat them to gain the sight I need. Once I've done that, their effects should last for a couple of hours. That should give me enough time to get into the cavern and collect a piece of discarded tusk. But before I can do that, I need to take the revived tassel plants back to the Brog, in the hope we can befriend him. We still have a couple of daylight hours this afternoon, so what do you think Ash? Do you think we could get this done today?'

'Great work Tilly! That's just brilliant. How did you find out what to do with the yarrow flowers? Oh, never mind, we haven't got time to chat, you need to get going, if we want to get this done today. You understand that I need to stay here, don't you? I can't bear to face that horrendous beast.' Ash scrunched his wrinkly face only to stretch it once more and smile his cheeky smile.

Returning a brave grin, Tilly got prepared. She placed the old trowel into her backpack (knowing she would need it to dig in the tassel plants for the Brog) and, with backpack secured over her shoulders and four healthy plants ready to go, there was only one thing left to do. Waiting on the workbench was the yarrow concoction. The crushed flowers lay there looking uninviting. Tilly stared at the unruly spread reminding her of a pile of weeds, which she guessed, they really were. Trying to imagine a plate of egg, chips and beans – one of her favourite meals, she picked up the first limp stem, with a grimace. Bringing it towards her mouth, she couldn't help but notice the distinct smell. It was like cabbage and didn't make her keen to eat it. But she had no choice.

Ash jumped up next to the yarrow ensemble and watched. His fidgety nature persisted as he shuffled and hopped around. Trying to concentrate, Tilly got irritated, 'Will you please stop Ash, I need to try and eat these things now!'

Still glancing down at him, she hesitated to place the first stem into her mouth. But closing her eyes as she began to eat it, as she chewed, Tilly discovered it tasted more and more like her favourite meal. *How strange,* she thought. Feeling puzzled, she tried another and to her delight, the flavours of her favourite meal became stronger and stronger. The more Tilly chewed, the more the flavours of egg, chips and beans came through. Soon enough, the whole pile of crushed flowers and their stems had been consumed.

'Did they taste nice?' Ash asked.

'Yes, strangely they did. They tasted just like my favourite meal.'

Ash began to giggle, 'Oh that's good then,' he said, knowing he had managed, by a touch of alchemy, to turn the simple yarrow into the most enticing of dishes. Tilly smiled as she realised that perhaps Ash's hopping around did help her after all.

Moments later, with the four healthy tassel plants scooped in Tilly's arms, she piped up, 'Wish me luck then Ash,' and went on her way, walking from the hut in the direction of the cavern. Walking with care, to not drop any of the precious cargo, soon enough Tilly arrived at the area in front of the cliff face, at the exact spot where she had fallen earlier. She noticed the patch of ground where she had landed which had been uprooted with no sign of the final sapling which fell with her. Tilly secretly hoped the Brog had found the fallen sapling, knowing the desperate situation he still faced.

Standing all alone and feeling a little uneasy in the beast's domain, Tilly considered her next move. She had to replant the crimson tassels but she had no intention of planting them down the muddy track, as she knew they would not survive in the boggy ground. So, slowly and logically Tilly searched for the right spot, where the Brog could access them upon higher ground.

Close by, near the corner of the cliff face, she saw an area rich in greenery. Long majestic ferns waved their fronds in unison and woodland mosses were bunched neatly underneath. Almost like a spotlight, the sun shone down on this place which seemed nearly perfect as a new home for the plants, easily accessible from the cavern. Tilly decided the area would be just right for the plants and for the Brog to access.

Very aware of the task ahead, Tilly promptly retrieved the trowel from her backpack and began to dig, placing each plant carefully into its new home. As she positioned the final one, she thought about her next step. She needed the Brog to see what had been done for him, but with that came uncertainty. If he was disturbed in his cavern, she thought he might be volatile, and Tilly didn't want to be the one to face that. Yet she needed him to appear for her plan to work.

She called for Saffron and from behind a tree Rowan and Dill, Saffron's inquisitive brothers, popped out. 'Hello Tilly, can we help you?'

'I'm looking for Saffron. I need help to encourage the Brog from his cavern. He needs to see what's been done for him, but I don't mind admitting, it's a risky ask, especially as he could lash out at anyone or anything,' Tilly said.

'Leave it to us and just wait there,' said Dill. 'We shouldn't be too long.'

As the seconds passed, the sky darkened and there seemed to be a storm coming in. The strength of the wind had increased since Tilly had arrived and the woodland trees swayed like a rocking ship on rough sea waves. Tiny woodland insects dashed around racing to their places of safety and Tilly stood holding her waistcoat tightly around her chest, listening to the howling wind whipping up the forest floor.

Gradually, the Flint fairies' whispers could be heard. Quietly at first, but then as they got louder and louder Tilly noticed more of the graceful fairies swooping in and out of the cavern, in a similar fashion to bats. She braced herself for what was to come, taking deep breaths to find every ounce of courage needed as she tried to remain calm. Standing close to the newly planted crimson tassels, she watched the cavern entrance intensely. A gust of wind launched a pile of fallen leaves into the blustery air close by and her wayward hair obscured her vision just as she noticed movement at the mouth of the cavern.

The Brog, plodded out straight away with its huge snout leading the animal into the blustery air. It seemed to sniff and Tilly stood motionless and scared. With its regular plod, the beast turned its head from side to side as its overly large body swayed towards her. She felt like a target; the focus for the irritated creature and without anything to protect herself, she quietly and subtly stepped back a few paces. To reach her, the Brog would have to go past the crimson tassel plants first, so Tilly held her nerve and almost froze to the spot as the beast moved closer. With each clumsy step, she watched hoping with fingers crossed her plan would work.

At the same time, tiny patters of rain had started and the sky had almost turned black. Tilly barely noticed how cold she had become. The Brog powered along on his stocky legs, constantly sniffing and, to Tilly's delight, he stomped directly to the crimson tassels, where he immediately began to gorge on one.

Although Tilly no longer felt in immediate danger she was reluctant to move for fear of disturbing the beast from his much-needed meal. The rain began to come down much harder and Saffron appeared beside her, beckoning her towards the cavern.

'Is it safe? Won't the Brog come after me in there?'

'The Brog is having his first decent meal in ages. He was so weak and now you have presented him with food. Look, the only thing on his mind right now is eating to survive. Even if he does come back, he knows that you have helped him and will not harm him. He accepts and appreciates you, please come. Now is your chance to get some old tusk.' Saffron briskly returned to the mouth of the cavern, taking a cold and wet Tilly with her.

Entering the cavern bought instant relief from the pouring rain, which continued to drip down Tilly's soggy clothes. At first, as she looked into the depths everything remained black and she wondered whether the yarrow flowers' magic would work. She thought about the hunt for the discarded tusk which could be in any crevice or between any loose rocks and not being able to see in the dark would make the task almost impossible.

Being slightly impatient, Tilly began to crawl along the rocky floor, feeling with her hands as she went. As she did so, the effects of the yarrow began to work, 'Wow!' she exclaimed, 'It does work, I can see everything so clearly!'

After just a few seconds, her eyes had adjusted. It was almost like a bright light had lit up the whole cavern. Tilly began her search. Saffron and her brothers flitted around her as she negotiated the rocky surface, encouraging her every move. A short distance in, she came across a snug clearing. It looked like the sort of place where the Brog might sleep, so she looked there first.

It became surprisingly warm in the cavern and as Tilly searched, she appreciated how suitable the cavern was for both the Brog and the Flint fairies, who shared his space. Above Tilly's head, the irregular roof canopy provided little pockets of mini caverns, where the Flint fairies could shelter. For a moment, she began to daydream once more and imagine what it would be like to be a Flint fairy herself. She stepped back a little and dislodged a rock slightly and as it rested in a new position, she regained her focus on the task ahead. 'So where *is* the bit of tusk I need?' she said aloud.

Still on her hands and knees, Tilly attempted to scan every inch of the creature's sleeping quarters. The search became a rather smelly one as she tried not to think of the Brog's sleeping habits. There were bits of animal hair and other unmentionables derived from a wild beast. Tilly held her breath and manoeuvred around a cluster of large boulders, checking in-between each one, but realised she could not avoid the foul smell for long. On all fours, it was necessary to avoid kneeling on sharp stones or cutting her hands as she felt around, so Tilly needed to concentrate, particularly as she wasn't entirely sure what she was looking for. Having not met a Brog before, she imagined the discarded tusk might be like a piece of skin, a sort of opaque colour, although she could only guess.

As the search continued, Tilly's knees became quite sore and wiping her grubby face, she gave herself a pep talk, 'you must keep going, it will be here somewhere, don't give up, you can't! Think of Ash. He needs you. Come on Tilly ... COME ON!'

Saffron floated above Tilly's head and then came into view. 'Tilly, you are so close now, this is where it should be, but we can't find it for you or the Newid charm won't work. You have to understand that the person who read the scroll has to be the person who gathers each vital piece for the charm.'

With her energy levels diminishing, Tilly kept searching, through every cluster of rocks and behind every stone. Finally, something caught her eye, something with a faint shimmery surface. As soon as she saw it, she shivered with anticipation and excitement. *This might be it!* Moving closer, the object looked like rolled up tissue paper and as Tilly touched it, it felt papery and thin. She picked it up and gently stretched it to form a similar shape to that of the Brog's tusk. This was IT! Tilly had found it.

In no time at all, the piece of treasure had been packed carefully away in the backpack and Tilly stepped back out into the cold, unwelcome weather. The wind still howled and the rain fell torrentially. Through the dark, blustery shower, Tilly glanced towards the tassel plants and to her relief, the Brog was still there, drenched but devouring his fresh feast. He raised his head and looked back towards her, before hastily lowering his head once more.

In the darkened sky, Tilly allowed herself to panic knowing she needed to get home and get home quickly.

Muddy and drenched, she arrived at the back gate with her hair limp and dripping. The house had lit up rooms yet she did not know how she would get in without being noticed. Creeping into the back garden, Mum greeted her with a smile, from the door. For some reason Tilly felt her flintstone necklace in her jeans pocket – she had forgotten all about it since her fall from the cliff face. Thinking quickly, she dropped it on the pathway just as her mum spoke up, 'Tilly love, it's raining, come on in.'

'Yes, coming Mum, I'm just picking up my necklace from the path.'

'Have you had a good day? It looks as though you've crawled around the whole garden – the state of your clothes. You'd better go and get cleaned up.'

'OK Mum will do.' Tilly entered the cottage, flicked her soggy trainers off and scooted up to her room, glad that no more questions were asked.

What a day! After having a long soak in the bath, Tilly felt tired and hungry. Thankfully it was nearly supper time and Mum and Dad were already in the kitchen preparing the table for the three of them. Smells of spaghetti Bolognese filled the air for the second time in the last few days as she breathed it in deeply. It smelt amazing, apart from the bits of vegetables of course.

Sitting at the table with a large bowl of food in front of her, Tilly picked out the bits of aubergine and listened to her parents' plans. Their thoughts confirmed it might only be one more day at the cottage before they left for home. Mum and Dad just had to finish emptying the garage and the rest of the attic. Boxes of stuff were already piled up in the front room ready to go back home. As they talked, Tilly's mind worked overtime, she kept thinking about the scroll and whether she and Ash could get the charm completed in time.

'Are you listening Tilly? You seem a bit distracted?' Mum said, bringing her back to the conversation.

'Yes, I heard. It's just I'm going to miss this place. I've found there are a lot of things to keep me occupied and I have so many fun memories here.'

'Yes, I know there are; it's quite a special place isn't it, especially for a young girl like yourself? You can really immerse yourself in your imagination, just like I did at your age,' Mum said with a warm smile.

Tilly hadn't really thought about the times her mum would have spent there as a child before. It had been her home while she grew up, so of course she would be very attached to it. Tilly's mum reached out across the table to comfort her, placing her hand on Tilly's and as she did so Tilly noticed a sparkling silver pendant hanging around her neck. She had not seen it before and something about it intrigued her. It was the size of a fifty pence piece and almost square in shape, it had rounded corners and delicate silver threads twirling around the edges. But that wasn't what caught Tilly's eye; in the centre behind a glassy front, radiated a beautiful purple sheen which she immediately recognised as the indigo feather from the Arion bird. Trying to inconspicuously look more closely, Tilly saw that the centrepiece was a section of one of the special feathers.

Numerous questions began to scramble around Tilly's head. How *did* Mum have that necklace? What if she knew more about Whispering Wood than she had ever let on? Did Mum *know* where the feather had come from?

Tilly promptly left the supper table, too nervous to ask any of the questions directly. She knew she could not jeopardise breaking the trust of the secretive realm by asking strange questions and she had no desire to uncover the reality of Ash and all the other amazing species she had met. Tilly knew, even if she wanted to, she could not ask her mum those questions.

Tilly spent the rest of the fading evening quietly in her room. With the possibility of only one more day at the cottage, it was imperative that she and Ash completed the charm to secure his future. Tilly also knew, the group of nine saplings of the crimson tassel kind, needed to be rehomed before her work was done.

Trying to clarify the day ahead, Tilly's eyes scanned her notebook, revisiting everything in minute detail, in preparation for the day ahead; a day Tilly felt could be incredible yet harrowing, still a day, nevertheless, she knew she must complete.

CHAPTER SIXTEEN

The Unplanned Event

At first light, in complete contrast to yesterday's eventful end, the day broke calmly. Tilly could not sleep and having awoken early, she lay motionless in the dark waiting for the dawn to break. As the autumn sun began to rise, she absorbed the delightful birdsong and observed fresh streams of light beaming into her room through the small wooden windows. After a time of quiet contemplation, Tilly jumped out of bed and reached for her notebook. There was so much to think about with her mind still crammed with thoughts for the day ahead, almost certainly the last day in the magical realm.

Making sure she had a good breakfast; Tilly did the final checks in her backpack. She must have checked at least three times to ensure the precious piece of tusk was still in there, ready to be transported safely back to the other collected ingredients within the hut.

With a heavy heart, Tilly assumed this would be the day she had to say farewell to her incredible friend, the beautiful Ash. She had formed quite an attachment to this imp-sized chap and although she wanted to succeed, she also knew by doing so she would have to say goodbye. Having mixed emotions about the day, Tilly felt the urge to give him a present. She wanted him to remember their time together, the challenges they faced and the empathy she had for him and his amazing secretive species.

Tilly decided to give him one of the Polaroid photographs and she reached into her waistcoat pocket. 'Of course,' she thought, 'there's the one with Grandad's microscope and one of the Fidgets! That *had* to be the one,' she thought. To acknowledge the emotional connection she felt with Ash, giving him the poignant picture felt the right thing to do. Its significance showed without question, the possible partnership between two species from two different worlds and it seemed very apt as her gift.

With the photograph all packed Tilly's nerves about the day ahead, began to surface. Her parents had already set off towards the garage so leaving the security of her room, she made her way to the back gate. As she stood to reflect, wearing her usual attire of denim jeans and casual top, with her explorer waistcoat over, she noticed a cooler breeze in the air, so returned to the back of the kitchen door to grab her bomber jacket. Back at the gate and standing very still, Tilly took in a few slow, deep breaths. She had no idea what she might face but she knew her role was pivotal in the success or failure of Ash's safe return to his family.

With composure and determination, Tilly embarked on her final journey towards the central glade. She chose the most direct route, taking her along the meandering path by the caverns once more. With purposeful steps, she passed the cavern face and began making her climb towards the glade. The storms overnight had caused some destruction leaving the forest floor difficult underfoot. As she continued, Tilly stepped over some small dislodged rocks onto the muddy pathway and as she did so, she slipped. In a matter of milliseconds, she landed quite hard on a bed of rocks. 'Ow!' she yelled. 'My leg!' Grasping her right leg above the knee, she felt immense pain and throbbing from her injured thigh. Even her jeans could not protect her and a large rip clearly showed the bloody gash beneath.

For a few traumatic moments Tilly held her leg tightly and rolled from side to side in severe pain. A combined faintness and overwhelming nausea came over her. Tilly needed help; there was no question of that. As she lay quite still, she heard movement nearby. Clutching her thigh, she raised her head a little to see what was there but the sight was not something she relished. The irritable Brog had come to investigate the commotion and the huge hairy animal was striding straight towards her. Tilly tried to shuffle away, but the pain was immense and she just couldn't move. With her rapid heartrate thumping in her chest, things began to go blurry and, in that instant, everything went black.

Tilly awoke as sparkly sprinkles rained down around her. She opened her eyes to see Sariel in touching distance, 'It's OK, do not move, we are getting help for you.'

'What happened?' she asked, not really aware of her surroundings.

'You fell and you are hurt – badly. Ash is on his way to help heal you,' Sariel said.

Tilly felt a warm presence behind her back, like a huge hot water bottle and feeling a little puzzled, turned her head slightly to see what it was. Her heart stopped. From the corner of her eye she saw the hairy skin of the Brog. 'I need to g … get away, please Sariel; help me!' she cried out in desperation.

'Do not fear, honestly Tilly, everything is fine. The Brog is your friend; he is keeping you warm until Ash gets here. He will not harm you. Please just rest and wait.'

Tilly could only wait. The deep gash in her thigh continued to throb and it took all her energy just to keep holding it. Beginning to cry, she thought of Ash and glimpsed impending failure. She could not see how the charm could ever get completed now; there were only a few hours left and so little time to achieve so much.

***

Back at the glade itself, a traumatised Ash scurried around in turmoil. It was clear he needed to face his worst nightmare; he had to leave the sanctuary of the protected central glade to not only save Tilly, but to also face the Brog. Considering his options, he had no choice; he had to do this to have any chance of ultimately saving himself.

Ash honestly didn't know if he could do it. In a complete melt down, he raced around his family tree, flapping his spindly arms in the air. He then paced up and down, mumbling to himself before crying out random words into the cool breeze around him. His behaviour would be attributed to an uncontrollable tantrum in a young child. After a few minutes, with his energy depleted, he collapsed beside the mystical stream and submerged his face. Soon enough, without air, he came back up spluttering and coughing before finally sitting more calmly on a comforting rock to compose himself.

Collecting his thoughts, Ash had to gather what he needed. He turned his attention to Tilly and knew, out of all the Fidgets, he had to help her, he was the *only* choice. He needed more yarrow plant and he needed water – the energising, healing water from his precious stream.

Ash wasted no more time in panic mode and quickly gathered the necessary resources into his foraging bag. He then focused on the other thing he needed, the newly nourished tassel plants which Tilly had retrieved from the cliff face the day before. Still within the dilapidated hut, the nine saplings had grown in stature and now proudly stood laden with an abundance of crimson foliage. Before placing each one into his magical foraging bag, Ash gave the roots a little more water. You could almost hear the grateful slurps as each plant soaked up their latest energised drink.

The time had come and Ash was all set. With thoughts of an injured Tilly uppermost in his mind, he continued to talk to himself, encouraging himself to venture from the safety of his central glade. He and his family had always stayed within the protective charm which covered the glade like a glass dome over a selection of cheese. Ash was so out of his comfort zone and had to push himself like never before. He knew, even though he feared for his life, he had to do it, to save Tilly, his new friend who he needed more than ever now.

Flying at 'imp speed,' the cliff face soon came into view. He slowed down and reached a gentle hover to pinpoint Tilly and the Brog on the ground below. As he made the gradual descent, Sariel kept watch and welcomed him warmly, 'Ash, well done, you are extremely brave, I know how much it must have taken for you to come here. You truly are a hero.'

Standing nearby, Ash tried to avoid any eye contact with the Brog and he felt like a quivering wreck. Looking at Tilly, his task rapidly came into sharp focus however, as her face was now very pale and she had become too weak to speak. With renewed motivation, Ash jumped onto his friend's hip and assessed the wound. A deep gash met with his concerned gaze. Tilly had lost a lot of blood. After reaching for the water from his bag Ash promptly began to pour some, a little at a time, across the angry wound. Placing the bottle down for a moment, he pressed his hand gently down onto the area and closed his eyes. He whispered some words – words only a Fidget with a special healing talent would know and seemed to meditate while the healing began to take place.

It wasn't too long before Ash lifted his hand to reveal a semi-healed wound. Things looked promising as he continued, until he became completely happy that the wound had resealed. Incredibly, Tilly's skin showed no sign of the previous injury. The only evidence of any previous gash was the rip in her denim jeans.

Ash checked the colour in her face. She appeared to be less pale now, although still extremely weak. Tilly opened her eyes and gave Ash a small, yet appreciative smile and with that he visibly drew a breath. It looked like she was going to be fine. Ash reached for the yarrow and placed it gently in her mouth, for her to chew. He knew it would encourage the healing process even more and help to restore Tilly's strength.

With work still to be done the plucky, headstrong imp scanned around to find a suitable place for the crimson tassel plants. After spotting the others near the cavern entrance and racing against time, Ash zipped over and without even looking back used his big bony hands as trowels, one by one, the whole batch were very soon settled in their new home.

With the job complete, Ash's shaky feelings began to take hold and his tiny frame quivered increasingly until the shaking seemed quite uncontrollable. Maybe adrenalin had kept him going till then. The poor, shocked imp felt so far out of his comfort zone it was impossible to explain as he faced his life-long fear of meeting the ferocious Brog.

As he still trembled a warm hand scooped him up. It was Tilly's hand. She raised him up towards her face and placed a gentle kiss upon his tiny head. Ash curled up within her palm and seemed to want to close his eyes. If he did he would keep them closed until they were back in the safety of the glade, but Tilly had other ideas. She turned around to face the Brog, who stood close by, watching her carefully with his beady eyes. She walked towards him and opened her palm, enough for Ash to see clearly. 'Ash, you must look, we couldn't have done this without him, the Brog I mean, he is our friend, and he saved me from the cold. And now, you need never fear him again, he has all the food he needs. Look, Ash Look!'

Ash was scared, but he also needed affirmation for himself that he could face his ultimate fear. With Tilly's encouraging words, he slowly opened his eyes. The Brog sniffed Tilly's palm with gentle appreciation, then turned and walked back to his cavern. Terrified, yet immensely proud, Ash emerged slowly, from Tilly's palm. They both watched the Brog's retreat and appreciated his acceptance of them, realising the mutual respect that had occurred this magical day. For a moment, what they then saw left them in disbelief; another hairy snout appeared from just within the cavern entrance. Taking a second glance, Tilly and Ash could not believe the sight before them.

'Look Ash!' Tilly jumped so excitedly that he nearly fell from her hand, 'There's another Brog! It definitely is, look! So this species could survive after all.'

After enduring a sequence of events they did not want to repeat, the exhausted pair made their way, slowly and safely towards the hut – the familiar and welcoming, rather damp smelling hut. With their end target still in mind, they both still had a critical job to do and there was no time to waste, no time at all.

CHAPTER SEVENTEEN

The Making of the Charm

Placing Ash gently down onto the well-worn workbench under the window, Tilly said, 'Thank you Ash. I was really in trouble there.'

'To be honest, I thought you were in trouble too. But it's all OK now,' Ash replied.

'Can you believe what we saw, was that *really* another Brog?' Tilly said. 'Hopefully, now, all will be well with enough crimson tassels to keep them alive.' As she spoke, Tilly couldn't help but notice a forlorn Ash staring through the musky glass towards his family tree.

'*He must be feeling so lonely without his family around him*,' she thought and wondered if she should mention what she had seen through the binoculars. She really didn't know if it would be helpful or not or whether it might jeopardise the whole charm. Weighing things up, Tilly felt it best not to tell him and attempted to reassure with comforting words instead, 'It shouldn't be too long now Ash, you'll soon be back with your family, come on, let's get the scroll out and see what else needs to be done. I have the piece of tusk in here ready to go into the box for now.' Tilly showed Ash her backpack and hoped he wasn't feeling too down. She really wanted to tell him his family seemed safe and well, but couldn't risk it.

The pair placed the necessary flaky tusk next to the fungus stalk within the wooden box before taking a moment to peer at the scroll instructions once again. The first two major points had been achieved, 'So, let's see ...'

They both concentrated hard, carefully checking the words once more, '... a stalk of the deadly cap fungus – yes, got that; ... a piece of discarded tusk – yes, we've got that too. We also need a sprinkle of sparkling water from the central glade and lastly one piece of hair from the explorer undertaking this task – well, that's me, I guess. Isn't it Ash?' Tilly looked for verification from her tiny friend.

'Yes of course it is silly!' Ash said affectionately.

'So, there is not much to do now.' Tilly couldn't believe what had been achieved. 'Ash, we are nearly there!'

It seemed difficult to contain their excitement as Tilly took a turn jumping around, this time. She presented utter excitement through fancy dancing steps on the spot. It had been such a stressful morning and now, for the first time, it felt like they might create the charm, the all-important element which could transport Ash back to his family, wherever they might be now.

Diving into one of the cardboard boxes, Tilly came out with a plastic jug. It seemed perfect for the sprinkles of sparkling water they needed. In the same box, she gathered three little sample pots and squeezed them into her inside waistcoat pocket.

With both now very much in sync, the pair walked out towards the stream. Tilly marvelled at its beauty; it had a sort of intensity which she had not noticed before. With a delightfully clear flow, the water presented a deep turquoise hue from its depths, above which tiny ripples of current babbled along. The surface, covered in sprinkles of light, seemed to dance along occasionally negotiating a large rock, sending the flickering light to the sides.

Admiring the water, Tilly wanted to discover its source and felt the urge to trace its origin. It wasn't long before she found herself at the top of the glade, on slightly higher ground than the Fidgets' majestic tree. The flow of the stream had reduced to a trickle and appeared to emerge from a dense area of stones and moss. Tilly thought about the wonders of nature and knew that not far from where she now stood was another higher valley, so assumed the source of the stream was beyond her reach. Having satisfied her curiosity, she turned to head back, following the stream once more. As she did so, a frog with beautiful army-camouflage markings hopped over from the mossy patch beside the trickling stream. He paused to look at Tilly and they eyed each other for several minutes before he hopped away to dive into the deeper part of the stream. She reflected upon the enjoyable moment she had just witnessed as she followed the soothing stream back towards her friend.

Ash had been quietly watching and, as Tilly approached, he saw her tranquil expression. Everything seemed so calm after the traumas they had been through. He spoke in a gentle voice, 'The extraordinary stream has rejuvenated itself since the Brog's visit. It is back to its full healing powers. It's a very special stream, come on Tilly, let's do this!'

Tilly leant down and with the jug in her hand, submerged the whole thing. As she did so the water flow rapidly filled the jug and cascaded over her hand. She raised the jug and poured a little back, to allow for easier lifting, and placed it on a flat stone beside her.

Without any warning, all sight of Ash had gone. Looking around, Tilly found him back near the top of the glade. He appeared to be tidying a few bits of uprooted moss and lichen close to his family tree. 'I've got the water Ash,' she cried out to her focused friend.

Ash looked up, but then beckoned Tilly to him. 'This is important, I need to get these final bits done,' he replied. His behaviour was frenetic. He scurried around the roots of his old family tree with a worried look.

'What is the matter, Ash? I've got the water now; don't we need to create the charm?'

'I need to put these few bits in order. I must leave it tidy, if I am to leave. I know I must see my family again, but I have lots of happy memories here. Just give me a few minutes.'

Tilly didn't have to say anything, she understood his feelings of connection to this special place, as she felt it too, and she had only just been introduced to it. Sitting down on the spongy grass, she watched as he tidied and nurtured the last few bits of uprooted grass. Ash then moved a couple of tiny pebbles into their rightful place before standing on one to quietly observe its new position. Tilly made good use of the time to reflect on the incredible journey she had made in this most secretive realm. Feeling rather pleased with herself, she closed her eyes to savour the moment.

Very abruptly, something poked her forehead. There stood Ash, just a few inches from her face, with a big, beaming, mischievous smile, 'Let's play a game, come on Tilly!'

'Oh, OK. Shouldn't we go and make the charm Ash?'

'I want to enjoy the fun of the glade, just one more time before I have to leave. You understand don't you?'

Of course Tilly understood and readily accepted Ash's proposal. 'What are we going to play?' she asked.

'I'll hide and you find me, ready ... close your eyes, just for a second.'

Tilly did what she was asked, and within a second, she could not see any sign of Ash anywhere. She heard giggling in one area, but as soon as she approached, the giggling stopped and emerged somewhere else. Tilly skipped from place to place, with feelings of utter joy and in animated flora. Magically, the plants and pretty ferns had decided to join in with the game, as they swayed rhythmically in response to the giggles. Occasionally, as she searched, a tap on her shoulder would interrupt her flow, and when she turned to see, the playful pocket-sized imp would be gone once more. It soon became clear that Tilly could not match Ash with his super speed; he could just zip around unnoticed to reappear somewhere else close by. After a while, Tilly admitted defeat and they both collapsed in giggling contentment on the magical carpeted glade.

'What will happen to Saffron, Rowan and Dill and the rest of the Flint fairies Ash?'

'They will stay here, until such a time as they are needed elsewhere. Their family are together and they will remain to continue to protect the Brog and perhaps other vulnerable species from potential extinction,' Ash replied.

Getting a little chilly and thinking about the time ahead, Tilly considered the charm once more and as she began to stand to make a move in the direction of the hut, she felt some vibrations in the ground below. Initially the vibrations were hardly noticeable, but then, soon enough, a definite shaking of the mossy ground could not be dismissed. The shaking got so bad Tilly almost fell back to the ground as she nervously watched. Then her excitement increased as the familiar crumbles of earth began to erupt above the surface and a tiny pink nose came into view. 'Old Hooky!' Tilly screeched in delight.

'Yes, I'm so pleased you remembered me. It's been a while since we last met,' the mole said. 'You have done a good job, but it is not yet complete. You must continue. Ash's family need him. I may not see you again, but know this; the realm will now be a better place because of your help. The creatures here will always remember you, your grit, your determination and your kindness. I must go now Tilly, but so must you to ensure all your good work isn't undone.' And with that Old Hooky reversed into his crumbly tunnel under a shower of soil.

At that moment, aromas of the aniseed scent filled the air, which reminded Tilly of the treasures before her. The source of the intense smell came from the dense shrubs with the masses of miniature white flowers, swaying nearby. Tilly never did discover their name.

The time had come for Tilly to act quickly. She wanted to gather some final samples as reminders of her unique experience within the wood. Using the pots from within her waistcoat, it wasn't too long before three examples had been collected; the aniseed smelling plant, a piece of broken toadstool and a piece of feathery fern.

Ash had been waiting patiently and was ready. Things now seemed to be in place for the charm to be prepared. Tilly retrieved the jug of water from the flat stone beside the stream and they both aimed for the hut without a word.

With the deadly cap fungus and the piece of tusk now on the workbench, this was it. It was time to combine the ingredients, as directed by the scroll and make the specific Newid charm. Tilly placed the jug of water beside the tusk and retrieved the scroll, opening it up. No mistakes could be made. Being extremely careful not to miss one bit, she placed the stalk of deadly cap fungus and the piece of discarded tusk into a large container found within a cardboard box. Ash stood nervously on the side of the container, putting all his faith in Tilly's actions, but there was no getting away from the fact that things were tense. Tilly reached for the jug of sparkling water and began to pour just a little into the mix. She had no inkling of how much to add, as the instructions just said, 'add a sprinkle of sparkling water,' so, as she gingerly poured she hoped, and prayed, her estimated sprinkle would work out well.

A fine dewy mist began to appear. 'Look, Ash look! Something's happening!' as Tilly quickly referred to the next instruction. 'Be ready to add the final ingredient, your strand of hair. When the hair is added the charm will emerge ... ensure you catch it or all will be lost.'

A subdued panic began to rise inside. Tilly knew she had to keep it together to get this done. She plucked one strand of hair from behind her left ear and held it above the dewy mist, gazing at Ash. 'This is it Ash, are you ready?' But then in a moment of realisation, Tilly gasped. What was she going to catch the charm in? 'Oh, flipping heck,' she cried, 'I've not even got a container ready! The instructions say 'catch it or all will be lost' I need to find something!'

Tilly knew she had to add the strand of hair now, but needed to find a suitable vessel in which to catch the charm. She dived into a dusty cardboard box flinging the lid flaps open and scooping the contents in haste, urgently searching for something that would do. Finding nothing, she delved into another. With a bit of luck, she saw a collection of old jam jars of various sizes and she grabbed the nearest old glass jar. Quickly returning to the workbench, she took off the lid and thought fast. She plucked another strand of hair from her head, before watching it float into the misty mix.

Not having any idea what the charm might look like, both Tilly and Ash watched intensely, waiting for it to emerge from the mix. The dewy mist began to thicken and after a short pause sparkling bubbles hatched in the base. The spherical opaque bubbles began to fizz and pop like Tilly's favourite Space Dust sizzling candy. Then, as they expanded, they clustered together forming a deep emerald liquid which grew and grew, soon spilling over the edge of the large container. Unfortunately, as the liquid spilled onto the workbench, the flow increased and the main bulk from within soon followed, as if it were racing to crawl up the side and out of the container.

Ash immediately began to hop up and down, as a matter of urgency shouting, 'Tilly, Tilly that must be it, catch it now!'

Without hesitation, Tilly scooped the glass jar under the emerald flow and caught the majority of what was left. With the flow diminishing to tiny droplets, she breathed out a huge sigh, 'That was intense!' she said as she banged the lid onto the top of the jar and screwed it securely.

As the glass jar was placed onto the slightly wobbly shelf, the liquid slowly settled. As it did so, it sent slow, regular waves to the sides of the jar, with tiny sparkling bubbles racing to the surface from the depths within. After a few moments, the contents settled until only the occasional bubble movement could be seen and there sat the vital charm both Tilly and Ash had been striving to achieve ever since they met.

After a long pause for the achievement to sink in Tilly finally shouted, 'Ash, we've done it, we've *actually* done it!'

CHAPTER EIGHTEEN

Searching for Sariel

A few minutes passed before neither Ash nor Tilly spoke a word. With both staring at the almost glowing, magical elixir, the pair remained in a hypnotic state and observed the intensity of the emerald charm, with the occasional elegant sparkling bubble still rising to the top.

'We've made the charm Ash; we've *actually* made the charm! Very soon you will be with your family again.' Tilly's words emerged tinged with sadness. She knew she might not see Ash again once the charm had been used. She tried to remain upbeat, to hide from him how she felt and said, 'We need to find Sariel. She is the only one who can conjure the charm successfully. Ash? Ash can you hear me?'

Staring though the cloudy window once more, Ash appeared to be daydreaming. 'Sorry, did you say something?'

'What is it, Ash? What's the matter?'

'I must go to the glade; I have some unfinished work to do. It's important.' Saying this, he flew through the gap in the side of the door and made his way towards the glade. Tilly quietly opened the rustic door and followed her close companion. As she did so, she carried the glass jar containing the charm with extreme care. She didn't want to lose sight of the precious cargo, not even for a second. As she walked along the small pathways, which she had become quite accustomed to over the last few days, she realised the titanic wrench Ash was about to make. This energetic, enchanted glade had been his home for as long as he could remember. And now, he prepared to be transported somewhere completely new, somewhere completely unknown. 'Of course,' she thought, 'he must be full of worry and may doubt that it will even succeed, it's only natural to be anxious.'

Tilly sat down, quite close to a cluster of feathery ferns. Some of the fronds had begun to change from the lush green shade to vibrant autumnal browns mixed in with new reds and yellows of other nearby flora. Tilly thought about her first day in the glade when she witnessed a fern uncurling its leaves to reveal a blue flower head. She remembered her amazement as it began to speak and now, after all the events, she held dear the words which were still imprinted in her memory. Waiting for Ash, she whispered them gently, 'Remember to remember that you are part of the secret realm now and what you discover here; what you go through here; must always stay in your heart. There may be challenges ahead, but you must persevere, for the sake of the Fidget world and all that is part of it. Tilly, you are one of us now.'

Feeling immensely proud, Tilly continued to observe Ash. He spent a few minutes hopping from area to area, tidying twigs, stroking roots and sometimes just running his fingers through the leaves of particular plants. He then turned and faced his family tree. With broad spindly arms, he reached as far as he could to embrace the majestic, proud, trunk. He then turned around, dithered a little and sat down with his back leaning against the base of the tree. Tilly could sense a tear erupting from one of her eyes. Watching Ash had become quite emotional, as she watched him say goodbye to his much-loved home. But she also knew he could be so proud; his enduring love for nurturing the natural habitat could be witnessed everywhere, with such beautiful and thriving plant life all around. Ash had definitely achieved that much and more.

Allowing him more time, Tilly reflected on her time within Whispering Wood. More tears began to flow as if to verify the connection she had made to the incredible place. Just then, out of nowhere, an indigo feather floated to the ground, no more than a foot away. She immediately looked up for she knew without any doubt from where it had come. As she searched, the dense canopy of trees that surrounded her parted slightly and the impressive bird with the swan-like neck flew into view. Like before, the imposing creature landed just a short distance away. Only this time, it swiftly lowered its eagle-like head towards Tilly's reach. She gently patted Arion's head and as she did so, Ash rejoined her. Keeping her composure, Tilly slowly lifted her hand from Arion's noble head and allowed him to take flight once more.

'This is such an amazing place Ash. I will never forget it, ever since our magical meeting when I discovered Grandad's hut. So much has happened and I will not forget our friendship, thanks Ash.' Tilly then remembered the photograph she had picked to give to him and realised if she didn't give it to him now, it would be too late.

'Ash, before we find Sariel, I'd like to give you something. I'd like to give you one of the photographs I have, to take with you, wherever you go.' Ensuring the charm jar remained secure on the ground beside her, Tilly rummaged into her waistcoat pocket and pulled out the photograph she had chosen. She laid it on the spongy path beside her. 'I've considered my choice very carefully and I wanted to give you this, the picture showing the unknown Fidget standing beside Grandad's microscope. I thought it would remind you of your family's special connection with my grandad, a human being, an outstanding human being.'

Looking humbled, Ash stared at the photograph, 'Are you sure? Are you absolutely sure?'

'Of course I am, absolutely!' Tilly said. As the pair looked at the photograph together for the last time, damp patches still obscured the identity of the Fidget, but Tilly also realised another problem, a problem with the handover itself ... being only 6 inches tall, there seemed a significant practical challenge for Ash to receive the kind gift. Each Polaroid picture measured approximately 4 inches by 3 inches in size, causing logistical challenges for him to hold. Tilly hadn't even considered the problem until now. Ash seemed unperturbed, however, as his wide, mischievous grin grew across his face. Relying on a little bit of imp ingenuity, he scratched his knee, wiggled his small misshapen nose and tapped the photograph three times. He then stepped right onto the photograph itself.

'Don't do that, you'll damage it even more!' Tilly shouted.

'It's OK Tilly, just watch.'

Tilly held her breath in anticipation as she watched him complete a series of manoeuvres like a funny dance. The photograph then began to light up, more and more, until it resembled a bright torchlight, just for a second before shrinking beneath his bony feet.

'What's just happened? Where's the photograph?'

'Here it is!' Ash responded. And as he lifted his foot from the ground a small square object appeared. Now tiny, about the size of a postage stamp, he lifted it carefully from the ground and nodding to acknowledge Tilly's kindness, he placed it into his foraging bag. 'Thank you, I will treasure it and who knows, I might even discover who the mystery Fidget is one day.'

Looking around, the daylight had begun to fade and Tilly felt a little uneasy. They still hadn't successfully implemented the transportation charm, which was the task they had been aiming to do ever since they met. 'Ash, we need Sariel and we need her now.' With one hand on the charm jar, Tilly lifted Ash into the air with the other.

'I have no control over Sariel. She just appears when she wants to. We will just have to wait.'

'If she doesn't arrive soon, it'll be too late, as I have to get home.'

With the fading light and the cooling sky, they waited and waited some more. Through the gaps in the surrounding trees, a few stars began to blink in the darkening sky. With the afternoon racing towards a picturesque sunset, a noticeable coolness began to whip around the glade. Just then, familiar gusts took Tilly by surprise and a sharper gust shot past her shoulder before a shower of illuminated sparkles rained down. With increased intensity at the next gust Sariel had finally arrived.

'Where have you been? It's getting dark and we didn't think you were coming.' Tilly felt exasperated yet relieved.

'I had to wait until the fading light. In these circumstances, it's the optimum time for the charm to work. Ash, are you ready?' Sariel asked.

As he fiddled with one of his eyebrows, he responded, 'I'm ready.'

The delicate, yet strong butterfly whipped up the air around the uneasy imp. Leaves from the autumn flora scrambled through each other as they surged to regroup at every waft. A mini tornado developed with Ash standing at the core. Sariel's wings acted like wands controlling the flow, then, just for a moment, her wings diverted and expanded to somehow engulf the jar and the charm within. The emerald liquid shot into the space above Ash's head and as it did so it formed an animated ring which moved continuously. He looked up to see a swirling magical ring, like a portal above his head. It felt comforting to him and he seemed transfixed on its motion.

'It's time,' Sariel said.

Strangely, as the swirling air and the mini tornado persisted, the noise it produced subsided just in time for Tilly to hear Ash say, 'Thank you, thank you all.' Moments later, the emerald charm intensified sending out a rainbow of colours all around and as it glowed Ash floated up and disappeared through its magical portal.

The mini tornado fell to the ground as the eclectic mix of leaves resurfaced upon the disrupted glade. But then, an incredible sight, Tilly's eyes could not avoid; all the plants came alive in their own unique way. They danced to show off their vibrant colours like a multi-coloured blanket comforting the earth. Across the grassy carpet, other magical flowers popped up to display their stunning heads in a show of unity before retreating into the earth below. The air filled with tiny orange orbs of energy which danced around like a bubbling ballet of exquisite form. Tilly stood in awe at the complexity of life around her, and took a moment to realise her faithful friend, the solitary Ash, had gone.

Standing alone, Tilly looked around. She took a couple of steps towards the stream and leant down to dip her fingertips into the refreshing water. The flow burst with life as her fingers tickled the tiny torrents going by. She felt sure the watery sparkles had intensified and as she stared into the depths of the stream, she glimpsed a light; a sharp piercing coloured light. Tilly stared, not flinching. It was as if the light had halted her every move as it beckoned her to explore further. She reached for the strangely controlling object and pulled it from its resting place. With pretty cascades of dripping water falling from her fingers, she looked closely at the object. On one side, she saw a motley appearance, not dissimilar to all the other pebbles at the bed of the stream, but on the other side the rock revealed its true treasure; a deep blue gemstone which twinkled at every turn. 'Wow!' gasped Tilly. 'What an amazing find.'

With the last light almost gone Tilly got moving and she dashed back to the hut. She had one more thing she needed to do. She quickly gathered the rest of the smooth pebbles that had been beside the old plant pots, before taking a moment to pause, with one more glance at the beautiful glade.

With a clear focus, Tilly headed off on her task. She picked up the pace and ran awkwardly, with the weight of the pebbles, to the base of the upright tree; the ember tree; the 'Arion' tree. Tilly wanted to place every other pebble, apart from the one she possessed, for the magical elusive bird to collect. It felt necessary to thank the majestic bird for his help in the quest. Concentrating, she continued on her way, making a quick pit stop at the crimson tassel plants to check their growth. But she needn't have worried as each one had multiplied and looked extremely healthy. She did not have to worry about the Brog either. Taking another short pause past the cavern itself, to see if any Flint fairies were around, she kept going through the dark where she safely reached her grandad's cottage.

'Now I'm nervous,' Tilly thought. 'It's nearly completely dark, what *will* my parents say?' She entered the garden as quietly as she could. She felt her hearing may have been playing tricks on her because as she did so she felt sure she heard the whispers once more, only this time, she could make out what was said. 'You did it Tilly. Well done. We thank you.'

All the house lights were on. Tilly crept along the back path and reached the back door without a sound. Not knowing what to say if greeted, she gradually pushed open the door, just enough to slide in sideways. She peeped into the kitchen on the left. Amazingly, with no sign of anyone close by, she tiptoed towards the stairs and crept up them. With huge relief, she found herself back in the safety of her room and amazingly no one had seen her arrive home.

Knock knock, came the sound from the door. 'It's only me, would you like a drink love, you seem to have been up here for such a long time.'

'Oh, um yes please Mum thanks,' Tilly replied, as she tried to look casual sitting on her bed.

'We've had a busy day; we've managed to finish sorting the garage and the rest of the attic, so it looks like we can head home tomorrow. You'll see there's not much room in the front room now, it's full of boxes,' Mum said.

'I'll come down for my drink Mum, as I'm a bit hungry too.'

'Great, well I've made a casserole, it's been cooking slowly all day in the Aga, so there's plenty to eat. I'll see you in a minute then.' And with that Mum disappeared downstairs and Tilly just couldn't believe her luck.

CHAPTER NINETEEN

Going Home

'Tilly, it's time to wake up. The van has arrived and your dad and I will be loading up the boxes in a while. Come and get some breakfast, I've made porridge,' Tilly's mum shouted through the bedroom door.

Even though Tilly had missed her alarm once before, it was not usual for her to do so, but today she had done so again. She glanced at her watch to see it approaching 9am and as she sat up, rubbing her eyes, she wondered if maybe, just maybe, she had been in some weird yet magical dream.

It didn't take long before her uncertainty went as she reached for her waistcoat to put on. There from the top pocket poked the indigo feather; the feather which had floated down upon the glade beside her, just the day before. Checking inside her backpack also revealed the smooth pebble she had discovered in the hut. And the photographs she held so dear would be a constant reminder of her incredible journey, which had now, it seemed, ended.

Tilly sensed her experiences of the last few days had brought about personal change. She felt braver than she used to and she also felt more confident. In a way, she felt the last few days had altered her desires and motivations for her future. She felt sure that she might want to help world conservation in some way. With the concern of global warming and the burning of fossil fuels producing acid rain, she constantly worried about the state of streams and rivers and how they may become uninhabitable for many species. She wanted nothing more than to one day, become a proper scientist just like her grandad.

Sitting at the kitchen table, Tilly ate her porridge and washed up the bowl and spoon straight away to pack into a box.

'Can you help us to load up some boxes Tilly?' Mum said walking into the room.

'What time do you think we will be leaving?' Tilly asked.

'Probably around late morning, maybe lunchtime, if you can give us a hand that would be great and then you can have some time to say your farewells to the place. I know you have some great memories here, as do I,' said Mum.

And with that, Tilly aimed for the front room to help. She chose the smaller, more manageable boxes and without haste transported them through the front door and along to the awaiting van. After about an hour, she needed a rest. Physically, her arms and the rest of her body had burnt off the porridge-produced energy and were now aching. She grabbed a drink of lemonade from the only remaining bottle on the kitchen side and helped herself to a digestive biscuit from the open packet. Feeling optimistic,

Tilly opened the fridge for a tub of cheese spread, as she loved the taste of cheese spread on digestive biscuits. Her optimism however dropped like a heavy stone as the interior of the fridge gleaned with emptiness – only half a pint of silver topped full cream milk for the emergency cups of tea.

Hearing clattering noises above, Tilly climbed the stairs to find the noises coming directly from her room. Mum and Dad were on their knees dismantling her ornate, iron-framed bed.

'Did you know love, this was my bed many years ago?' Mum announced, as she removed yet another strut from under the mattress.

'No, I didn't know that, but it would make sense as I guess this was your bedroom as a child,' Tilly replied.

'Yes, it was. I will miss the place, but now Grandad is sadly no longer here, we will have to sell this cottage pretty soon.' Lifting the iron side bars Mum and Dad, headed for the stairs. As they left Tilly noticed Mum's silver pendant once more. With the morning light just catching it, the piece of indigo feather was clear to see. She really wanted to ask so many questions, but could only manage one. 'Mum, I like your pendant. Where did you get it from?'

'It was a present from your grandad one year for my birthday. It's pretty isn't it?' Before Tilly had a chance to reply, her mum continued, 'When Dad and I have removed your bed, could you check your room to make sure it's completely empty please?' With that, Mum followed Dad down the stairs holding the end of the iron bars.

Tilly had already dismissed any idea of Mum knowing anything about the Arion bird now. After all Grandad had given it to Mum as a gift, so why *would* she know anything. With a quick glance and only the hefty iron headboard and the mattress to go, there didn't seem to be anything left in the room. A few minutes later, with the headboard and mattress gone the room stood empty and Tilly puzzled over what Mum had said.

What did she mean by making sure it's completely empty? Looking around, with no furniture left within the room, it was indeed completely empty, other than Tilly's backpack which rested beside the door. Yet she felt uneasy, perhaps hesitant; something was telling her not to leave the room. Tilly sat down against the wall and propped her arms across her knees. From the corner of her eye, she noticed a faint glow coming from her backpack once more. She opened it up, reached inside and there, once again, the smooth pebble was glowing. She took it into her hand but this time she quickly lost grip and the pebble rolled along one of the squeaky floorboards before coming to rest near the other side of the room.

'That was strange,' Tilly thought. She was just getting up to retrieve the pebble when the floorboard it rested on lifted a little. Tilly gasped and feeling a little scared, carefully approached the other end of the floorboard. She could just about get her fingertips into the gap, but before she did so she noticed the floorboard was particularly short; it had been cut across just a few inches away, like a separate small piece from the main board. Without dithering any longer, Tilly gripped the end of the board and began to pull upwards. A few squeaky seconds later, the board came up quite easily and revealed a dark cubby hole underneath. Inside, apart from a couple of cobwebs, there lay what looked like a book.

A thick layer of dust covered the top, but unruffled Tilly lifted it up and out. The mysterious book seemed to be leather-bound, brown in colour, quite plain and a little tatty around the edges. Tilly raised the book and blew the layer of dust from the top, causing a wave of shimmering particles in the shards of daylight which gradually fell to the floor. Gently rubbing the front, she could see there were no words, just a couple of small patches of mould. Immensely intrigued and without delay, she opened the book and on the first page she immediately recognised Grandad's spiky handwriting. The page contained random notes about plants and a roughly sketched map. With excitement building, Tilly turned the pages, one by one, to find more notes about plants and unusual samples, which lead her to assume she had discovered his record book or a general notebook for his botany notes and scientific research.

Enthralled by every page, Tilly kept turning them, sheet after sheet. Most of the notes were too difficult to read and she would need much more time to establish what they said, but on every few pages there were rough sketches which helped.

'Tilly, are you nearly ready up there? We have to be going fairly soon,' said Mum, shouting up the stairs.

Tilly jumped as she heard Mum's voice. Being so enthralled by the discovery of the book, she had forgotten the time. 'Yes, I'll be down now,' she responded.

Closing the book, she placed it carefully into her backpack alongside the precious binoculars she had discovered in Grandad's hut. She also retrieved the smooth pebble from the floor and then reinstated the small section of floorboard, pushing it down and standing on the edges to ensure it fitted snuggly back into place.

The time had come to say a fond farewell to the cottage and Tilly took one last look around her room and headed for the stairs. She didn't want to miss the opportunity to spend a few minutes in the back garden. The garden held many happy memories where she had spent many hours, being guided and taught numerous skills by her dear grandad. Strangely, the seconds seemed to slow down to allow Tilly the breathing space to reflect on her precious time spent. She found herself just resting on the flaky back gate and staring into Whispering Wood. As she did so, she touched her special piece of flint attached to her bootlace necklace. She thought about Saffron and the Flint fairies and then Ash, hoping he had been reunited with his family, wherever that might be. She reflected upon the time she looked through the binoculars and witnessed seeing Ash's family huddled together and hoped he had arrived safely back with them.

Tilly imagined seeing him again one day, but sensed her wish may be a wish too far. Nevertheless, as long as he had been reunited, then she could be proud of that.

With the final goodbye getting ever closer, Tilly concluded the events of her time and she pondered more on why Ash was left behind, so brutally separated from his family. Perhaps, she wondered, it formed part of a bigger plan to enlist her help, to not only help him and the Fidget species, but to also restore a healthy balance of plant life to sustain other creatures, such as the Brog.

Tilly reminisced over the complexities and problems she had faced with tiny Ash by her side and then the feelings of jubilation as the transportation charm worked causing such a dynamic, celebratory reaction across the glade. To her, it really felt like the whole experience truly *did* awaken and present the magical diversity in the secretive woodland, showing just how precious all the life forms were.

A huge sense of accomplishment came over Tilly and as she stared into the depths of the wood a tiny Flint fairy peeped around the edge of a tree and winked before disappearing into the dark beyond.

With the van fully loaded, Dad sat in the driving seat waiting to leave. Tilly decided to accompany Mum in the family car. With the cottage all locked up, a sad aura hung in the air and she considered whether she would ever return to this magical place. Then she climbed into the front seat of the car. She placed her backpack next to her feet, guarding it tightly as it held her precious belongings, including the newly discovered book and the mystical binoculars. With her seatbelt on, Tilly looked up at the cottage for the last time. It looked cold and empty, yet somehow, she could feel the spirit of her grandad still there. As Mum drove quietly away, neither she nor Tilly said a word. It seemed they both needed some quiet time to reflect. A few minutes from the cottage, Tilly thought about the dusty book she had discovered and wondered who had left it there for her to find. Maybe it was Grandad's hideaway place, she thought. Tilly also considered whether Mum knew of its whereabouts, after all, thinking it a little strange for her to say what she had about checking the room was completely empty.

A few miles later, Tilly reached into her waistcoat pocket to look again at the precious photographs she held. Pulling them out, she placed them on her lap and lifted the first one. It showed the unusual saplings within the hut with the clusters of smooth pebbles resting beside the pots. Tilly smiled as feelings of pride filled her whole body, knowing she, petite shy Tilly, had helped to restore the equilibrium within the mystical woodland. She thought about the magical orbs she witnessed as the glade came to life and she felt sure the natural balance within the glade had been restored. Yet, across the planet, there was still so much to do to prevent humans continuing to destroy such natural environments.

Tilly closed her eyes with sadness about whether she would ever see Ash again. The friendship they shared; she knew she would miss terribly. Thinking philosophically though, she understood that in life, change was a constant and so she would just have to accept it if their paths did not meet again.

With at least another half an hour travelling time before getting home, Tilly opened her eyes just briefly to witness one of the pebbles in the photograph light up, subtly at first before gradually beaming brighter and brighter. She cupped her hand around the image to avoid her mum's glance and, trying to remain calm, she felt excitable bubbles churning over in her stomach. After such an incredible adventure, perhaps it was not over after all …

The Last Fidget is the first book in the forthcoming
The Endearing Fidgets Series